Aligote to ZINFANDEL

Exploring the World of Wine

Other Wine Books by the Author

The Wine Lover's Companion
Cellar & Silver (with Rose Murray)
The Dinner Companion (with Jacques Marie)
Vintage Canada
Tony Aspler's International Guide to Wine

Fiction
Blood Is Thicker than Beaujolais: A Wine Lover's Mystery
Titanic
The Music Wars (with Gordon Pape)
The Scorpion Sanction (with Gordon Pape)
Chain Reaction (with Gordon Pape)
One of My Marionettes
The Streets of Askelon

•

Aligoté to ZINFANDEL

Exploring the World of Wine

Tony Aspler

McGraw-Hill Ryerson

Toronto • Montreal

Copyright © 1994 Tony Aspler

First published in 1994 by
McGraw-Hill Ryerson Limited
300 Water Street
Whitby, Ontario
L1N 9B6

Canadian Cataloguing in Publication Data
Aspler, Tony, 1939-
    Aligoté to Zinfandel: a beginer's guide to wine appreciation

Includes index.
ISBN 0-07-551675-6
1. Wine and wine making.   I. Title.

IP548.A7   1994   641.2'2   C94-932001-3

Publisher: Donald S. Broad
Cover design: Dave Hader, Studio Conceptions
Cover photograph: Steve Elphick
Text design: JAQ
Editorial services provided by Word Guild, Markham, Ontario.

This book was produced for McGraw-Hill Ryerson by Shaftesbury Books, a member of the Warwick Publishing Group, Toronto.

Printed and bound in Canada

To Deborah

ACKNOWLEDGEMENTS

When I sit down to write a wine book, my first instinct is to consult experts and specialists in the field, either in person or through their writings.

For *Aligoté to Zinfandel*, I started with consumers who enjoy drinking wine. I wanted to find out what kind of information they thought would enhance their enjoyment of wine.

To this end, I witnessed focus groups held by the Liquor Control Board of Ontario and Seagrams (thank you for allowing me to sit in) and I held one of my own. I am grateful to Alice and Joanne Durst, Kate Hall, Nadine Melemis and Susan Zwickel who — prompted by my curiosity and an endless supply of red and white wine — shared their ideas on what the ideal book for the wine novice should contain. I'd like to thank them for their guidance and good humour, and trust that I've been faithful in following the direction they provided with such conviction.

I would also like to acknowledge a debt of gratitude to the late Heather Somerville of McGraw-Hill Ryerson who helped keep me on the right track during the initial stages of this project and who beat the drum so effectively for my other books over my long association with MHR.

Contents

Chapter 7: Wine and Food • 75

Chapter 8: The 20 Questions Most Asked of Wine Professionals • 95

Introduction

*W*ine can be very simple, or it can be very complicated. It's all a matter of approach.

If you're keen to know the sugar levels of the grapes at harvest, the amount of Total Acidity and the pH of the wine, what type of French oak the Cabernet Sauvignon was fermented in or whether the wine was fined with diatemaceous earth or egg whites, then you can make the study of wine complex enough to satisfy a geneticist.

But if you enjoy the idea of pulling a cork and pouring a glass to share with friends, and you'd like to know what different wines taste like and what foods complement these tastes, then all you need to keep in mind are the basics.

Aligoté to Zinfandel is about the basics. As the title suggests, it's an easy-to-follow A to Z guide to wine. The book is aimed at people who would like to understand wine, but don't quite know where to start.

Nothing can be more bewildering than to walk into a liquor or wine store (or be dining out) and see row upon row of labels from all around the world. What wine do you choose and how will you know what it tastes like before you open it? Will it be dry or sweet? Will it be full-bodied or light in the mouth? What's the best way to serve it? What dishes does it suit and what foods should be avoided? These are the kind of questions you would like to have answers to before you commit yourself to buying a bottle.

Aligoté to Zinfandel will answer these and many other questions you may have about wine. Use it in good health. Cheers!

Wine Pronunciation Guide

*L*et's start with a glass of wine before we delve into all the business of what makes it taste the way it does and how to get the best value for your money.

In fact, let's order a bottle. If you're not sure of what to order or how to pronounce a wine name, you can always point to a wine on the restaurant wine list and say, "I'll have that one." But if you can ask for the wine by name, you already begin to feel like a connoisseur.

The problem is that many wine and grape names are unfamiliar and difficult to pronounce, so a pronunciation guide with the wine's geographic region follows.

WINE NAME	PRONUNCIATION	MAJOR REGION
Aligoté	Ali-got-tay	Burgundy
Auxerrois	Awks-air-wah	Alsace
Auxey Duresses	Awks-ee Dew-ress	Burgundy
Amarone	Am-ar-OWE-neh	Veneto
Anjou	Ahn-jhoo	Loire
Asti Spumante	As-tee Spoo-man-tee	Piedmont
Baco Noir	Back-o Nw'ar	Ontario
Bairrada	By-radda	Portugal
Banyuls	Ban-yulls	Roussillon

WINE NAME	PRONUNCIATION	MAJOR REGION
Beaujolais	Bow-jho-lay	Burgundy
Barbaresco	Bah-bar-ESK-o	Piedmont
Barbera	Bar-BARE-uh	Piedmont
Barca Velha	Bark-a Vale-ah	Portugal
Bardolino	Bard-o-LEAN-o	Veneto
Barolo	Bah-ROLL-o	Piedmont
Barsac	Bar-sack	Bordeaux
Bâtard-Montrachet	Bat-ar Mon-rash-eh	Burgundy
Beaumes-de-Venise	Bome-de-Ven-eez	S. Rhône
Beaune	Bone	Beaune
Bergerac	Bare-jher-ak	Dordogne
Bernkastel	Bairn-cast-el	Mosel
Blaye (Côte de)	Blay	Bordeaux
Bonnes Mares	Bon-Mar	Burgundy
Bonnezeaux	Bon-eh-zoh	Loire
Bordeaux	Bor-dough	Bordeaux
Bourg	Boor-gh	Bordeaux
Bourgogne	Boor-goyn-yh	Burgundy
Bourgeuil	Boor-goy-ee	Loire
Brouilly	Brew-yee	Beaujolais
Brunello di Montalcino	Brew-NEL-lo dee Montal-CHEE-no	Tuscany
Buzet (Côte de)	Booz-eh	S.W. France
Cabernet Sauvignon	Cab-ern-eh Sow-vin-yawn	Most regions
Cabernet Franc	Cab-ern-eh Frahnk	Most regions
Cahors	Kah-oar	S.W. France
Carema	Ka-RAY-ma	Piedmont
Carmignano	Kar-min-YAN-o	Chianti
Cérons	Sair-on	Bordeaux

WINE NAME	PRONUNCIATION	MAJOR REGION
Chablis	Shab-lee	Burgundy
Chambertin	Shom-bare-tan	Burgundy
Chambolle-Musigny	Sham-bowl Mew-sin-yee	Burgundy
Chardonnay	Shar-don-nay	Most regions
Chassagne- Montrachet	Shass-ang-ne Mon-rash-eh	Burgundy
Châteauneuf- du-Pape	Sha-toe-neuf-dew-Pap	S. Rhône
Chénas	Shay-nass	Beaujolais
Chevalier- Montrachet	Sheval-ee-eh Mont-ra-shay	Burgundy
Chianti	Key-an-tee	Chianti
Chiroubles	Sheer-oo-bluh	Beaujolais
Clos de	Clow de	"enclosed vineyard"
Clos de Tart	Clow-de-Tar	Burgundy
Clos de Vougeot	Clow-de-Vooj-oh	Burgundy
Colares	Coal-ar-esh	Portugal
Condrieu	Con-dree-uh	Rhône
Corbières	Cor-be-air	Languedoc
Cornas	Cor-nass	N. Rhône
Cortese di Gavi	Kor-tay-zee dee Gah-vee	Piedmont
Corton- Charlemagne	Cor-ton Shar-le-mine	Burgundy
Côte de Nuits	Coat de N'wee	Burgundy
Côte Rôtie	Coat Row-tee	N. Rhône
Côteaux champenois	Cot-oh shom-pen-wah	Champagne
Côteaux du Layon	Cot-oh dew Lay-on	Loire
Côtes de Roussillon	Coat de Rue-see-on	Rousillon

WINE NAME	PRONUNCIATION	MAJOR REGION
Côtes de Ventoux	Coat de Vant-too	S. Rhône
Coulée de Serrant	Cool-eh de Ser-on	Loire
Crémant d'Alsace	Cray-mont dal-sass	Alsace
Crémant de Bourgogone	Cray-mont de Bour-goyn-yh	Burgundy
Crozes-Hermitage	Crows-air-mit-ahge	N. Rhône
Dao	D'ow	Portugal
Dolcetto	Dol-CHET-toe	Piedmont
Debroi Hárslevelü	Deb-roy Har-slev-el-loo	Hungary
Echezeaux	Esh-ez-oh	Burgundy
Egri Bikaver	Egg-ree Bik-a-vair	Hungary
Entre-Deux-Mers	Ent-tra-duh-mair	Bordeaux
Erbaluce	Air-ba-LOO-chay	Piedmont
Fendant	Fon-dohn	Switzerland
Fiano di Avellino	Fee-AN-o dee Avel-LEAN-o	Campania
Fitou	Fit-two	Languedoc
Fixin	Fee-san	Burgundy
Fleurie	Flewr-ee	Beaujolais
Frascati	Fras-KHA-ti	Latium
Freisa	Fraz-ah	Piedmont
Gaillac	Guy-ack	S.W. France
Gattinara	Gat-in-AIR-a	Piedmont
Gavi	Gah-vee	Piedmont
Gevrey-Chambertin	Jev-ree-Shom-bare-tan	Burgundy
Gewürztraminer	Gev-ertz-tram-in-air	Alsace
Ghemme	Ghem-may	Piedmont
Gigondas	Jhig-on-dass	Rhône
Givry	Jiv-ree	Burgundy
Graves	Grah-ve	Bordeaux

WINE NAME	PRONUNCIATION	MAJOR REGION
Greco di Tufo	Gre-ko-Dee-Too-foe	Campania
Grignolino	Grin-yo-LEAN-oh	Piedmont
Griotte-Chambertin	Gree-ott Cham-bare-tan	Burgundy
Grumello	Groom-ELL-oh	Lombardy
Grüner Veltliner	Grew-ner Velt-lean-er	Austria
Haut-Médoc	Oat-May-dok	Bordeaux
Haut-Poitou	Oat-Pwah-too	Loire
Hermitage	Air-mit-aj	N. Rhône
Heurige	Hoy-rig-uh	Austria
Inferno	In-FARE-no	Lombardy
Juliénas	Jool-ee-ay-nass	Beaujolais
Jurançon	Jour-an-son	S.W. France
Lacryma Christi	LAC-ree-ma Kris-ti	Campania
Ladoix	La-dwah	Burgundy
Lambrusco	Lam-BROOS-ko	Emilia-Romagna
Languedoc (Côteaux du)	Lann-g'dock	Midi
Laticières-Chambertin	Latis-ee-air Shom-bare-tan	Burgundy
Lessona	Less-OWN-a	Piedmont
Liebfraumilch	Leeb-frow-milsh	Rhine
Lirac	Leer-ac	S. Rhône
Listrac	Lees-track	Bordeaux
Loupiac	Loo-pea-ac	Bordeaux
Mâcon	Mack-ohn	Burgundy
Madiran	Mad-ear-ohn	S.W. France
Malaga	Mala-gah	Spain
Marechal Foch	Mar-ay-shal Fosh	Ontario
Margaux	Mar-go	Bordeaux
Marsannay	Mar-san-eh	Burgundy

WINE NAME	PRONUNCIATION	MAJOR REGION
Mavrodaphane	Mav-ro-daff-an-eh	Greece
Mavroud	Mav-rood	Bulgaria
Mazis-Chambertin	Maz-ee Shom-bare-tan	Burgundy
Médoc	May-dok	Bordeaux
Ménétou-Salon	Men-ay-too Sal-on	Loire
Mercurey	Mair-cure-eh	Burgundy
Meursault	Muhr-so	Burgundy
Monbazillac	Mon-baz-ee-ack	Bergerac
Montagny	Mon-tan-yee	Burgundy
Montepulciano	Mont-eh-pul-CHIA-no	Abruzzi
Monthélie	Mon-tay-lee	Burgundy
Montrachet	Mon-ra-shay	Burgundy
Morey St. Denis	Mor-eh San Den-ee	Burgundy
Morgon	Mor-gon	Beaujolais
Moulin-à-Vent	Moo-lahn-ah-Vohn	Beaujolais
Moulis	Moo-lee	Bordeaux
Muscadet	Moosc-a-day	Loire
Musigny	Moose-ee-nhee	Burgundy
Naoussa	Now-oo-sah	Greece
Nebbiolo	Neb-ee-ollo	Piedmont
Nemea	Nem-ee-a	Greece
Nuits (Côte de)	N'wee	Burgundy
Nuits St. Georges	N'wee San Jhorj	Burgundy
Orvieto	Oar-vee-AY-toe	Umbria
Pauillac	Poy-yack	Bordeaux
Pécharmant	Pay-shar-mont	Bergerac
Periquita	Pera-keet-ah	Portugal
Pernand- Vergelesses	Pear-nan-Vare-jhel-ess	Burgundy
Petit Chablis	P'tee Shab-lee	Burgundy

WINE NAME	PRONUNCIATION	MAJOR REGION
Picolit	Pick-o-leet	Friuli
Piesporter	Peas-porter	Mosel
Pinot Bianco	Pea-no Bee-anko	Italy
Pinot Blanc	Pea-no Blahn-k	France
Pinot Grigio	Pea-no Grij-ee-o	N. Italy
Pinot Nero	Pea-no NAIR-o	Italy
Pinot Noir	Pe-no N'wahr	Oregon
Pomerol	Pom-air-rohl	Bordeaux
Pomino	Pom-EEN-no	Tuscany
Pommard	Pom-arh	Burgundy
Pouilly-Fuissé	Pou-yee-Fwee-say	Burgundy
Pouilly-Fumé	Pou-yee-Few-may	Loire
Prosecco	Pro-seck-o	Veneto
Puligny-Montrachet	Pou-leen-yee Mon-ra-shay	Burgundy
Quincy	Can-see	Loire
Rasteau	Ras-toe	Rhône
Recioto di Soave	Retch-ee-otto dee Suave-eh	Veneto
Recioto della Valpolicella	Retch-ee-otto della Val-pol-i-chello	Veneto
Regaleali	Reg-al-ee-all-ee	Sicily
Regnié	Rain-yay	Beaujolais
Retsina	Ret-seen-ah	Greece
Richebourg	Reesh-boorg	Burgundy
Rioja	Ree-o-ha	Spain
Romanée-Conti	Rome-an-eh-Con-tee	Burgundy
Roussanne	Rew-san	Rhône
Rubesco	Rube-esko	Umbria
Rully	Rew-yee	Burgundy

WINE NAME	PRONUNCIATION	MAJOR REGION
St. Amour	Sant-Am-oor	Beaujolais
St. Emilion	Sant-Ay-meal-eon	Bordeaux
St. Estephe	Sant-Ess-teff	Bordeaux
St. Joseph	San-Joz-eff	Rhône
St. Julien	San-Jhool-ee-an	Bordeaux
St. Péray	San-Pay-ray	Rhône
St. Romain	San-Rome-an	Burgundy
St. Véran	San-Vay-rhan	Burgundy
Ste-Croix-du-Mont	San-Cr'wah-dew-Mohn	Bordeaux
Sancerre	Son-sair	Loire
Santenay	Son-ten-eh	Burgundy
Sassicaia	Sass-ee-khai-yah	Tuscany
Savennières	Sav-en-yehr	Loire
Savigny-les-Beaune	Sav-en-yee-lay-bone	Burgundy
Sauternes	So-tairn	Bordeaux
Setubal	Sh-too-bal	Portugal
Schloss Johannisberg	Sh-loss-Yo-hannis-berg	Rheingau
Seyval Blanc	Say-val Blonk	Ontario
Sfurzat	S'fur-zat	Lombardy
Soave	Suave-eh	Veneto
Szeksardi	Sex-ard-dee	Hungary
Tache, La	Tash (La)	Burgundy
Taurasi	Tore-ass-ee	Campania
Tavel	Tah-VEL	Rhône
Teroldego Rotaliano	Tare-OL-day-go Rot-al-EE-ano	Trentino
Tignanello	Tin-yan-ELL-o	Tuscany
Tocai Friulano	Toke-eye Free-oo-LAN-o	Friuli
Tokay d'Alsace	Toke-eye dal-sass	Alsace

WINE NAME	PRONUNCIATION	MAJOR REGION
Tokay (Tokaji)	Toke-eye	Hungary
Torgiano	Tore-gee-AN-o	Umbria
Touraine	Toor-rain	Loire
Tricastin (Côteaux de)	Tree-cas-tan	Rhône
Vacquéras	Vak-air-rass	Rhône
Valdepeñas	Val-de-pen-yas	Spain
Valpolicella	Val-pol-ee-CHELL-a	Veneto
Valtellina	Val-tel-EEN-a	Lombardy
Vega Sicilia	Vay-ga-Sit-CHEE-lee-a	Spain
Verdicchio	Vaire-DEEK-ee-o	Marches
Verduzzo	Vaire-DOOT-so	Veneto
Vernaccia di San Gimignano	Vaire-NATCH-ee-o dee San-Jim-in-YAN-o	Tuscany
Vidal	Vee-DAL	Ontario
Vinho Verde	Veen-o-Vhair-day	Portugal
Vin Jaune	Van-jhoan	Jura
Vino Nobile di Montepulciano	Vee-no NOBE-ill-lay dee Mont-ay-pul-CHEE-anno	Tuscany
Vin Santo	Vin-san-toe	Italy
Volnay	Voll-nay	Burgundy
Vosne-Romanée	Vone-Rom-an-ay	Burgundy
Vouvray	Voove-rhay	Loire
Yquem (Château d')	Ee-kem (Shat-oh d')	Bordeaux
Zinfandel	Zin-fan-dell	California

CHAPTER 1

What Is Wine?

ine is the fermented juice of freshly picked grapes — *most of the time*. I say this because some people make an alcoholic beverage from fruits and flowers (elderberries, plums, rhubarb, dandelions, etc.) that they call "wine."

Also, sometimes the grapes used in winemaking are not freshly picked. In some wine-producing regions, the vintners won't press and ferment the grapes when they are newly harvested. The grapes will be dried on trays indoors for a few months in order to concentrate the grape sugars which will be used to make sweet wines.

But, for the purposes of this book, think of wine as the fermented juice of freshly picked grapes.

FERMENTATION

How much alcohol does wine contain?

Most wines contain at least 8 percent alcohol. Anything less than this amount of alcohol will mean the product is not really stable and will taste thin in the mouth. The average high-alcohol content in wine is 14 percent.

1

There are exceptions at both ends of the scale. The lack of alcoholic strength can be compensated by high acidity as in certain German Rieslings, and by natural grape sugar as in some Italian sparkling or still Muscat wines that can have an alcohol content as low as 5 percent.

Certain wines from warm growing regions can have an alcoholic strength of 16.5 percent if the grapes are dried before fermentation.

How is alcohol produced?

When grapes are crushed, their juice is released. When this juice comes into contact with yeast, a fermentation starts: the natural grape sugar is converted into alcohol giving off a by-product of carbon dioxide gas. This gas usually disperses into the air. If any CO_2 gets bound into the wine, it will give a slight prickling sensation on the tongue. (This happens quite often with Beaujolais Nouveau, Muscadet and certain northern Italian white wines.)

Why does one wine contain more alcohol than another?

The amount of alcohol in the finished wine depends upon the amount of sugar in the grapes at the time of harvesting. Low grape sugars will mean low alcohol; grapes that are rich in natural sweetness will be high in alcohol. (Unless, of course, the fermentation is stopped before all the sugar has been converted to alcohol. This will leave residual sugar in the wine.)

Grapes grown in warmer climates will generally have more sugar than those grown in cool climates. Sunshine, direct or indirect, builds up grape sugars. (Cool nights build up acidity.) For instance, a wine such as Châteauneuf-du-Pape grown in the southern Rhône Valley will have higher alcohol than a Beaujolais grown in southern Burgundy because of the amount of sunshine the respective regions enjoy during the growing season. The French wine law recognizes this fact of Nature and states that for a red wine grown in Beaujolais to be labelled as such, it must contain a

minimum of 9 percent alcohol. Châteauneuf-du-Pape, on the other hand, must have a minimum of 12.5 percent alcohol.

Grape Sugars

A wine grape contains between 15% and 25% sugar depending on the variety and how ripe it gets. These carbohydrates are mainly glucose and fructose which can be fermented.

Fresh grapes also contain pentose — another form of sugar which because of its molecular structure cannot be fermented — so there will always be some residual sugar in the finished wine.

Can a winemaker artificially boost the alcohol content in a wine?

In poor or mediocre years in many wine regions of the world, winemakers will add granulated cane or beet sugar directly to the crushed grapes before or during fermentation to increase the amount of alcohol. These sugars will usually augment the alcohol content by 1 or 2 percent.

This practice of adding sugar is called *chaptalisation* after Napoleon's Minister of Agriculture, Baron Jean-Antoine Chaptal, who first sanctioned the process in France although it had been practiced for centuries. The Romans used to add honey to their fermenting wines to build up the alcohol.

Cold climate wines by definition will contain less alcohol than those grown in hot climates. German wines grown at the northern limit of grape production are generally low in alcohol. Some German Rieslings grown in Mosel, for example, contain as little as 7 percent alcohol. Contrast this with southern Italian reds that can register as high as 16 percent alcohol.

Comparison of Alcoholic Strength

Beverage	Percent of Alcohol by Volume
Pure Water	0
Beer	2–8
Table Wine	8–14
Sparkling Wines	5–14
Fortified Wine	15–22
Liqueurs	20–55
Spirits	40–45

SPIRITS are made by distilling a "wine-like" liquid usually containing approximately 7% alcohol.

LIQUEURS are spirits that have been flavoured with fruits, herbs, spices or other botanicals and then sweetened.

FORTIFIED WINES are wines that have grape or grain spirit added, usually to stop the fermentation (as in sherry or port).

What effects does alcohol have on wine?

Alcohol is a great preservative. As an antiseptic it will kill certain bacteria. It will also allow the wine to age without deteriorating if the bottle is properly cellared.

Alcohol also gives the wine weight and substance: the higher the alcohol content, the heavier the wine will feel in the mouth. Although alcohol has no smell, you can detect high alcohol con-

tent by the thickness of the residue left on the side of the glass when you swirl it. The heavier the "tears" that fall back to the surface of the wine, the higher the alcohol.

High-alcohol wines will also give the sensation of heat when you smell them and you can feel hotness in the mouth and throat.

SWEET AND DRY

What makes a wine taste dry?

Basically, it is the acidity that makes a wine taste dry. Wine contains a number of acids including citric (the same as lemons) and malic (green apples). Unripe grapes or grapes from young vines will be contain higher acidity than ripe fruit from mature vines.

Acidity is very important to wine. Without sufficient acidity you would only taste the sweetness of the fruit. It would seem flabby and without structure. Acidity defines the wine and prolongs the flavour on the palate.

What do Sugar Codes tell about a wine?

Not as much as you think they do. A wine that is rated as zero (0) will have up to 0.49 grams per litre of residual sugar.

> Sugar Code (1) 0.5 – 1.49 grams per litre of residual sugar
> Sugar Code (2) 1.5 – 2.49 grams per litre of residual sugar
> Sugar Code (3) 2.5 – 3.49 grams per litre of residual sugar
> etc.

Certain wines that are rated as zero on the Sugar Code will have very different tastes in terms of their sweetness. Lindeman's Chardonnay Bin 65 from Australia is rated as (0); so too is Sauvignon Blanc de Haut Poitou from the Loire Valley. But, if you compared them side by side, you would find the French Sauvignon Blanc tastes like a tart grapefruit whereas the Australian Chardonnay tastes of sweet oak and butter.

The driest champagnes are rated as (1) on the Sugar Code, but

they will taste drier than most table wines rated as (0) because of their high acidity.

What determines the perception of dryness in a wine is the amount of fixed acidity (the different fruit acids — citric, malic, tartaric, lactic, etc.) and its pH — the measure of the intensity of this acidity. The lower the pH of a wine, the sharper the wine will taste.

The pH of lemon juice is around 2.3. Dry wines will range from 2.8 to 3.3. A Muscat from a warm growing region will have a pH close to 3.95. A wine with this high a pH will taste soft and rather flabby. Connoisseurs would say such a wine lacks acidity.

Is there a totally dry wine?

In a word, no. The yeast will not ferment grape sugars to zero sugar. Some sugars are unfermentable so there will always be a minimal amount of sweetness left once the fermentation has stopped. This could be as low as 3 grams per litre. But high acidity will make certain wines taste as if they have no sweetness at all.

What the Sugar Code Indicates

(0) is the driest style of wine. Examples: Most Chardonnays, Cabernet Sauvignon, Soave, Chianti.

(1) to (2) is a wine with some residual sugar, not sweet but definitely on the fruity side (what the trade refers to as "off-dry"). Examples: Blended table wines, German dry wines, Vinho Verde, Portuguese rosés.

(3) to (4) is semi-sweet. Examples: Blush wines, Late Harvest Riesling, German Spätlese.

(5) to (6) is sweet. Example: Dessert wines.

(7) to (10) is very sweet. Examples: Cream sherry, port.

However, if you have a glass of Ontario Icewine, the amount of acidity is so high that it balances the residual sugar and stops the wine from cloying. The acidity refreshes the palate.

How are sweet wines made?

1. By allowing the grapes to get super-ripe on the vines after the normal harvest (late harvest wines).
2. By adding lavish quantities of sugar to the grapes prior to fermentation and then stopping the yeast to ensure residual sugar in the wine (old-style Kosher wines).
3. By drying the harvested grapes in boxes or on mats to concentrate the grape sugars (Vin Santo, Recioto della Valpolicella).
4. By adding brandy or neutral spirits to the fermentation to kill the yeast (sherry, port).
5. By allowing the grapes to freeze on the vine and pressing the frozen bunches (Icewine).
6. By fermenting a wine to dryness and then blending back 10 percent to 25 percent of unfermented grape juice (widely practiced in Germany where they call it *Süss-reserve* or sweet reserve).
7. By filtering out the yeast during fermentation before it has finished converting the grape sugars to alcohol.
8. By allowing the grapes to be attacked by *Botrytis cinerea*, a noble rot that occurs in warm, humid conditions. The fungus punctures the skins of certain grapes and allows the water to evaporate, thus concentrating the sugars and acids. (Examples: Sauternes, German Auslesen, Beerenauslesen and Trockenbeerenauslesen).

WHEN BUYING WINE

What will the wine I want to buy taste like?

Many people buy the same wine every time they go to the liquor store because they know what it tastes like and they don't want to be surprised or disappointed by spending money on something new that they may not like. This is a shame since there are literally hundreds of wines from all around the world, each with its own distinctive taste, that ought to be enjoyed.

The simplest way to judge what a wine will taste like without pulling the cork is to play wine detective. There are certain things you can learn about a wine without having to pour it into a glass. All you have to do is to read the label (and the back label, too, if the bottle has one).

To determine what a wine will taste like, ask yourself the following questions:

What is the wine's alcohol strength?

The alcohol content will tell you about how the wine will feel in the mouth. Will it be light, medium-bodied or full-bodied?

    light-bodied (8% by volume – 10% by volume)
    medium-bodied (11% – 12% by volume)
    full-bodied (12.5% – 14% +)

What is the grape variety or wine name?

Each wine grape has its own distinctive taste. For a profile of what bouquets and flavours you can expect from specific grape varieties, see Chapter 2. For specific wine names, see Chapter 3.

Where was the grape grown?

A Chardonnay grown in Chablis will taste very different to one grown in Chile or California. The climate and soil have a bearing on the ultimate flavour of the wine.

In general terms, cool climate growing areas (as in Northern Europe, Ontario, New York, New Zealand) will produce wines that have higher acidity levels than wines from warm or hot growing regions such as California, Australia and Chile. Warmer climates provide ripe (high sugar) grapes which produce higher-alcohol wines with greater concentration of fruit and lower acidity.

So expect wines from cooler regions to be leaner and lower in alcohol than wines from warm growing regions.

What is the wine's vintage?

The vintage date tells you the year grapes were harvested and crushed. In the northern hemisphere, the harvest happens usually

in September or October; in the southern hemisphere, March or April.

In regions such as California and Australia, there is not much fluctuation of temperature from one year to the next. The vintages are more even than they are in northern Europe where there can be dramatic disparities in temperatures from one year to the next.

Each region has its own climate which can vary significantly within its own borders. For instance, an early summer hail storm in Burgundy can move across the vineyards and destroy one farmer's grapes while leaving his neighbour's intact.

A vintage chart (see pages 108–109) will give you a broad indication as to what the overall quality of the year was for a given region. However, it cannot take into consideration what individual winemakers did. One grower may have picked his grapes just before a rain and made a stunning wine, while others in the village may have left their crop on the vine hoping for a week of sunshine for extra ripeness. The rain would be sucked up by the vine's roots, swelling the berries and diluting their sugars. The wine from such grapes would be thin.

The presence of a vintage date gives you the age of the wine. It will appear either on the label, on the neck label or the back label.

The absence of a vintage date suggests that the wine is a blend of two or more years.

Most white wines should be consumed within two years of the vintage date. Most reds should be consumed between two and five years (for budget and medium-priced wines), and six to ten years (for quality wines).

Is the wine the product of a single vineyard or village?

By determining where the grapes were grown for a specific wine, you will get some idea about its quality.

In the wine world, small is beautiful. The smaller the area the grapes come from, the better the wine will be. Even within a single vineyard there will be a parcel of vines that produces the ripest, healthiest grapes. Most winemakers will isolate these grapes and ferment them separately to make their most

expensive wine. (These may be called "Reserve" wines, although there is no international convention setting out a definition of reserve.)

Grapes do not ripen at the same rate. Vines at the bottom of the slope will not get as much exposure to sunshine as those at the top. They won't be as well drained and may be more susceptible to frost damage or vine pests. Grapes on individual bunches, too, will ripen at different times. Usually the ripest part of the bunch is the outer top corners which have more exposure to the sun. (The Italians call them *recie*, meaning ears. Recioto della Valpolicella is a wine made from these fully ripened clusters.)

In most cases, a single vineyard wine will be superior to a wine that has a village appellation. (Example: A wine from the village of Beaune in Burgundy will not be as good as Beaune Clos des Mouches which comes exclusively from the vineyard of that name.)

Comparatively few wines you will find in most liquor stores originate in a single vineyard. Most will be a blend of different vineyards from the same village or region. Just keep in mind that, in general terms, the larger the geographic area, the lower the quality will be.

How deep is the colour?

White wines start off life as water white. They gain colour as they mature, especially those aged in barrels. Sweet whites will be deeper in colour than dry whites.

Red wines in their youth are purple. As they age they lose colour, running through a spectrum of ruby to garnet and beginning to turn brick-coloured and orange at the rim and eventually brown. The depth of colour and its hue can give you an indication about how the wine will taste.

While it is not easy to determine the colour of a red wine through green or brown glass, you can get some idea of it by holding the neck of the bottle up to the light. You will certainly be able to see if the wine has intensity of colour or not. Red wines that you can see through will not have the same concentration of flavour as those that are opaque.

In white wines, a pale, almost water-white wine will mean a light, crisp, dry wine which has probably been fermented and aged in stainless steel as opposed to oak (for the effect of oak, see below).

A golden wine suggests either richness of flavour, long maturity (look at the vintage date) or sweetness.

Was the wine barrel-aged or barrel-fermented?

Most wines today are fermented and aged in stainless-steel tanks. These tanks, which can be as large as 100,000 litres or more, are inert and airtight. Stainless steel adds nothing to the wine, maintaining the true flavour of the grape and its freshness.

The use of oak barrels changes the flavour of wine. First, barrels "breathe" through their staves allowing the wine to come into contact with air. Oxygen ages wine and the properties of the wood add the taste of vanillans and the feel of wood tannins.

The size of the barrel, too, can influence the amount of oak taste the wine absorbs. Small barrels will impart more oak flavour than large barrels and new barrels more than older barrels.

If the label says the wine was fermented or aged in French or American oak barrels, you can expect the wine to have the bouquet and taste of oak. Depending on where the oak originated, the taste will be of vanilla or coconut with a spiciness reminiscent of cloves, cinnamon or mace.

Oak is more widely used on wines from warm growing regions because they have the fruit extract that will support the additional taste of the wood. The more delicate flavours of wines grown in cool growing climates might be overpowered from being aged in oak.

Is there sediment in the bottom of the bottle?

A fine dust-like deposit in a bottle of red wine is a testimony to its age. The sediment is tannin and colouring matter that has been precipitated out over the years. If stirred up this sediment will make the wine muddy and will also introduce a bitterness to the taste. The bottle should be carefully decanted to separate the wine from the sediment. (See Why Decant?, page 87.)

For expensive old wines, use a coffee filter on the heel of the bottle so that you don't waste precious wine.

What size is the bottle?
The size of the bottle has a direct bearing on how fast the wine will mature. A bottle of red wine that may still be closed and tannic because it is too young could be more drinkable in the half-bottle format. The smaller the amount of wine in a container, the faster it will mature. Magnums (1.5 litres) take longer to mature than bottles. So, if you want to cellar red wines to celebrate an anniversary a decade or more in the future, choose the magnum size.

What is the condition of the label and the capsule?
When buying wine, make sure that the label and the capsule are in good condition. A scuffed, stained label suggests a badly stored wine and that could mean a disappointment when you pull the cork. A wine that has been badly handled, exposed to excessive light, heat or vibration will be oxidized and taste like stewed prunes and mushrooms.

Avoid leakers. If the capsule shows that wine has gotten out of the bottle, it means that air can get in and the wine will smell like vinegar. Ensure that the cork is just below the lip of the bottle or flush with it. If it protrudes, the wine has been subjected to heat and could be "off."

How full is the bottle?
Winemakers fill their bottles to within half an inch to an inch of the cork. Air is the enemy of wine, and too much will make it go "off." With age some wine will evaporate and the air pocket between the cork and the wine will increase. This is called "ullage." It is dangerous to the wine's health. When buying wine, select bottles that have a good fill.

How are wines labelled?

Wines are labelled in one of four ways:

1. By the grape variety. Examples: Chardonnay, Cabernet Sauvignon, Gewürztraminer, Pinot Noir.
2. By the village or region or estate or vineyard where the grapes were grown:

   VILLAGE – Vouvray, Barolo, Pommard

   REGION – Chianti, St. Emilion, Chablis

   ESTATE – Château Lafite-Rothschild, Pomino, Schloss Johannisberg

   VINEYARDS – Sassicaia, Richebourg, Corton
3. By a fantasy or brand name which suggests a blend of different wines. Examples: Liebfraumilch, Sangre de Toro, Belle-Ami.
4. By a shipper or producer's name. Examples: Calvet Reserve, Kressmann Selectionné, B&G Cuvée Speciale.

   Labels will also contain the following information:
1. The producer's name and address.
2. The designated appellation of the wine.
3. The vintage date (either on the label, a neck label or back label). If there is no vintage date, assume that the wine is a blend of at least two vintages.
4. The name of the wine or grape variety and its quality.
5. The name of the vineyard, if applicable.
6. A generic description (e.g., Dry White Table Wine).
7. Alcoholic strength measured as a percentage by volume.
8. Liquid contents measured in millilitres (750 ml in a bottle) or centilitres (75 cl).
9. The country where the wine was grown.
10. In some jurisdictions a warning that the product contains sulfites (see pages 44-45).

Moselland eG

White wine

1991
Bernkasteler Kurfürstlay
Riesling
Qualitätswein
A.P.Nr. 2 576 260 050 93

Vin blanc

750 ml
Product of Germany

9.0% alc./vol.
Produit d'Allemagne

+035675

MOSEL-SAAR-RUWER
MOSELLAND eG WINZERGENOSSENSCHAFT
D-5550 BERNKASTEL-KUES

CRU BOURGEOIS

CHATEAU LE CARDONNAT

GRAND VIN DE BORDEAUX

1988   1988

MIS EN BOUTEILLE AU CHATEAU

HAUT-MÉDOC
APPELLATION HAUT-MÉDOC CONTROLÉE

ROBERT GONZALVEZ
PROPRIÉTAIRE A ST-SEURIN-DE-CADOURNE - GIRONDE - FRANCE

Jordan

ESTATE BOTTLED
1989
Chardonnay
Alexander Valley

GROWN, PRODUCED & BOTTLED BY JORDAN VINEYARD & WINERY
HEALDSBURG, CA · ALCOHOL 12.5% BY VOLUME · CONTAINS SULFITES

LUNGAROTTI

RUBESCO
1990

CHAPTER 2

Grapes and Their Flavours

*T*here are some 8,000 different grape varieties, but there are only one hundred or so that are of interest to wine lovers. Being able to identify the taste of a grape by name will give you an idea of the style of wine it will make.

Grape	Type white/red/rosé	Drink young/mature	Taste	Wine
Aligoté	*	*	crisp, citric	Aligoté
Aglianico	*	*	rich, tarry	Taurasi
Alvarinho	*	*	fresh, light	Vinho Verde
Auxerrois	*	*	acidic, medium	Auxerrois
Bacchus	*	*	floral, off-dry	Bacchus

(Note: "ss" designates fermented or aged in stainless-steel tanks)

Grape	Type white	red	rosé	Drink young	mature	Taste	Wine
Baco Noir		*			*	smoky, blackberry	Baco Noir
Barbera		*			*	medium, acidic	Barbera
Bual	*				*	sweet Madeira	Bual
Cabernet Franc			*	* (pink)	* (red)	violet, raspberry	Cabernet Franc
Cabernet Sauvignon		*	*			blackcurrant	Cabernet Sauvignon
Carignan		*		*		powerful, acidic	blending grape
Chardonnay	*			(ss)	(oak)	apple, tropical fruits	Burgundy
Chasselas	*	*				fresh, citric	Fendant
Chenin Blanc	*			(ss)	(sweet)	apple, acidic	Vouvray
Cinsaut		*		* pink)	* (red)	heavy, peppery	S. Rhône
Colombard	*			*		soft, flowery	Colombard
DeChaunac		*			*	acidic, smoky	DeChaunac
Dolcetto		*			*	black cherry	Dolcetto
Dornfelder		*			*	smoky plum	Dornfelder
Ehrenfelser	*			*		aromatic, floral	Ehrenfelser
Emerald Riesling	*			*		crisp, fruity	E. Riesling

Grape	Type white/red/rosé	Drink young/mature	Taste	Wine
Friesa	*	*	light, raspberry	Friesa
Fumé Blanc	*	*	dry, grassy	Fumé Blanc
Furmint	*	*	toffee	Tokay
Gamay	*	*	fruity, cherry	Beaujolais
Gewürz-traminer	*	*	aromatic, lychee	Gewürz-traminer
Grenache	* *	(pink) (red)	powerful	blending
Gignolino	*	*	light, grapey	Gignolino
Grüner Veltliner		*	acidic, fruity	Grüner Veltliner
Hárslevelû	*	*	spicy, aromatic	Hárslevelû
Johannisberg Riesling (*see Riesling*)				
Kerner	*	*	fruity, aromatic	Kerner
Malvasia	*	*	sweet, perfumed	Malvasia
Marechal Foch	*	*	peppery, plummy	Marechal Foch
Marsanne	*	*	heavy, peachy	N. Rhône
Mavro-daphne	*	*	sweet, plummy	Mavro-daphne
Merlot	*	*	black-berry, black-currant	Merlot
Morio-Muscat	*	*	spicy, grapey	Morio-Muscat

Grape	Type white/red/rosé	Drink young/mature	Taste	Wine
Mourvèdre	*	*	rich, black-berry	blending
Müller-Thurgau	*	*	soft, floral	Müller-Thurgau
Muscadelle	*	*	sweet, perfumed	blending
Muscadet	*	*	crisp, green fruits	Muscadet
Muscat	*	*	sweet, perfumed	Muscat
Nebbiolo	*	*	truffles, violets	Barolo/Barbaresco
Palomino	*	*	neutral, soft	Sherry
Petite Sirah	*	*	peppery, blackberry	Petite Sirah
Picolit	*	*	medium sweet	Picolit
Pinot Blanc	*	*	light, appley	Pinot Blanc
Pinot Gris	*	*	peachy, rich	Tokay-Pinot Gris/Ruländer/P. Grigio
Pinot Noir	*	*	raspberry violets	(red Burgundy)
Pinot Meunier	*	*	red berries	blending acidic (Champagne)

Grape	Type white/red/rosé	Drink young/mature	Taste	Wine
Pinotage	*	*	heavy, plummy	Pinotage
Primitivo	*	*	spicy, blackberry	Primitivo
Riesling	*	(dry)(sweet)	floral	Riesling
Ruby Cabernet	*	*	light black-currant	Ruby Cabernet
Sangiovese	*	*	violets, acidic	Chianti
Sauvignon Blanc	*	*	grassy, goose-berry	(Fumé Blanc)
Scheurebe	*	*	aromatic, fruity	Scheurebe
Sémillon	*	*	tart, green plum	white Bordeaux
Sercial	*	*	green fig	Madeira
Seyval Blanc	*	*	grassy, green plum	Seyval Blanc
Shiraz	*	*	spicy black-berry	(Syrah)
Silvaner	*	*	mild, acidic	Silvaner
Steen	*	(dry)(sweet)	apple, acidic	Steen (Chenin Blanc)
Syrah	*	*	black-berry, pepper	(North Rhône)

Grape	Type white/red/rosé	Drink young/mature	Taste	Wine
Tempra-nillo	*	*	straw berry	(Rioja)
Trebbiano	*	*	acidic, lemony	Trebbiano
Verdelho	*	*	soft, nutty	(Madeira)
Verdicchio	*	*	crisp, acidic	Verdicchio
Vernaccia	*	*	dry, herby	Vernaccia di San Gi-mignano
Vidal	*	*	acidic, fruity	Vidal
Viognier	*	* *	peach, quince	(Condrieu)
Viura	*	*	acidic, fruity	(white Rioja)
Welsch-riesling		*	floral, zesty	(Riesling Italico)
Xynomavro	*	*	dark, fruity	Xyno-mavro
Zinfandel	*	*	powerful, black-berry	Zinfandel

THE MOST POPULAR GRAPES

Cabernet Sauvignon (red):
Produces long-lasting, deeply coloured red wines that are astringent when young but mellow with age. As red Bordeaux, particularly from the Médoc and Graves regions, the wines are leaner and more elegant that Cabernets grown in California, Australia or Chile.

Noted flavours: Cedar and blackcurrant.

Chardonnay (white):
Makes a dry wine whose range of flavours depends on where the grapes were grown and how long the wine stayed in oak (if at all). Chardonnay will be labelled as such in most regions other than France where it is named after the village where it was grown. Examples: Chablis, Meursault, Montrachet, Pouilly-Fuissé.

Champagne also uses Chardonnay in the blend and exclusively as Blanc de blancs Champagne.

Noted flavours (cool climate): Apple, vanilla, nutty; (warm climate): Tropical fruits, smoky, spicy.

Chenin Blanc (white):
The wines can range from very dry to off-dry to sweet as well as sparkling. Best known as Vouvray and Saumur (villages in the Loire Valley). Also grown in California which makes a softer, less acidic wine, and in South Africa where it is frequently called Steen.

Noted flavours: Pear, apple.

Gamay (red):
The grape of Beaujolais. Makes a light, fruity wine that can be consumed young, especially chilled. When blended with Pinot Noir in Burgundy, the wine is called Passe-tout-Grains.

Noted flavours: Cherry, pepper.

Gewürztraminer (white):

The most unforgettable of grapes. Grown in Alsace and Germany and throughout Europe as Traminer, the wines have an exotic perfume of lychee nuts, rose petals and sometimes red peppers. They suggest sweetness on the nose, but the best (from Alsace) are dry. Also produced in Oregon and California and Ontario. *Gewürz* is German for spicy, and *Traminer* means from the town of Tramin where the vine was first propogated.

Noted flavours: Lychee, rose petals.

Merlot (red):

Very similar to Cabernet Sauvignon but softer, fruitier and faster-maturing. In Bordeaux and in many other regions, including California, it is blended with Cabernet to make the wine rounder. Merlot predominates in St. Emilion and Pomerol, producing dark, full-bodied wines.

Noted flavours: Blackberry, blackcurrant.

Muscat (white, less commonly black):

Although it is made as a dry wine in Alsace and sometimes in Australia, Muscat wines are generally sweet and rich. They are usually grown in warm climates; the hotter they are, the sweeter the wine will be, culminating in the Muscat of Samos (Greece). Black Muscat is invariably a sweet dessert wine.

Noted flavours: Grapey, aromatic.

Nebbiolo (red):

Grown extensively in Piedmont and other northern Italian provinces, Nebbiolo produces the long-lived, somewhat austere Barolo and Barbaresco with their characteristic bitter finish.

Noted flavours: Truffle, tar, roses.

Pinot Blanc (white):

Similar in character to the Chardonnay, it is generally broader in flavours. Grown extensively in Alsace. The Italians call it Pinot Bianco, and it is widely used in sparkling wines. In Germany it's

the Weissburgunder. Generally low in acidity.
Noted flavours: Apple, peach.

Pinot Gris (white):

One of the most underrated of grapes, grown mainly in Alsace where it is called Tokay-Pinot Gris. In Italy it's called Pinot Grigio; in Germany and Austria, Ruländer. Full-bodied white with lots of flavour. Some of the best come from Oregon.
Noted flavours: Peaches.

Pinot Noir (red):

A notoriously fickle grape. When fully ripe makes exquisite wines in Burgundy that age almost as long as red Bordeaux. Also successfully grown in Oregon and California. Extensively used in the production of Champagne (where it is blended with Chardonnay). When used by itself, it is called *blanc de noirs* (a white wine from black grapes.)
Noted flavours: Raspberry, strawberry.

Riesling (white):

Perhaps the most versatile white wine that can range in style from steely dryness to honeyed sweetness. The bouquet is floral with a freshness from the acidity. It grows best in cool climates and reaches its apogee in Germany. Best wines come from Mosel and Rheingau in Germany, Alsace and Washington State.
Noted flavours: (Dry) lime, grapefruit; (Sweet) honey, apricot.

Sangiovese (red):

The major grape in Chianti (along with Canaiolo) although now Italian producers are beginning to make it a varietal wine. It is 100 percent in Brunello di Montalcino and a constituent of Vino Nobile di Montepulciano. Highly acidic and tannic.
Noted flavours: Cherry, truffle.

Sauvignon Blanc (white):

This grape smells of grass, pea pods and elderberries. It is best known for the wines of the Loire, Sancerre and Pouilly-Fumé. It grows well in California, too. In Bordeaux it is blended with Sémillon to produce such wines as Entre-Deux-Mers. Generally dry and crisp, it can make a sweet late harvest wine with good acidity.

Noted flavours: Gooseberry, fig.

Sémillon (white):

Not often used as a varietal, this grape is generally blended with Sauvignon Blanc to make dry white Bordeaux. Similar in style to Sauvignon Blanc, but more floral and not as herbaceous. Sémillon is the major grape in the sweet wines of Sauternes and Barsac.

Noted flavours: Fig, green plum.

Syrah (red):

Makes the powerful, rich dry wines of the Northern Rhône (Hermitage, Côte Rôtie) and is a constituent in the blend of Châteauneuf-du-Pape and the wines of the Southern Rhône. Ages well. Also grown successfully in California. In Australia, it is called Shiraz where it makes a varietal wine and is also blended with Cabernet Sauvignon.

Noted flavours: Blackberry, pepper.

Tempranillo (red):

The major red grape of Spain where it is also called Ull de Llebre. Has long aging capabilities and produces wines that remind you of both red Burgundy and red Bordeaux.

Basic flavours: Strawberry, spices.

Zinfandel (red):

Native to California, this grape is used to produce off-dry blush wines for immediate consumption as well as powerful dry reds for aging and port-like dessert wines.

Noted flavours: Blackberry, raspberry, spices, pepper.

CHAPTER 3

Wine's Taste Components

Wines can be classified by how they taste and how they feel in the mouth. Taste is not only the sweetness of the grapes — or lack of it. It is also a combination of acidity, tannin and oak, and the sensation of weight in the mouth — how heavy or full-bodied it feels.

We experience sweetness on the tip of the tongue which means that our first impression of a wine may be sweet although it could finish as very dry and crisp, as in some German Rieslings.

Since we taste sourness (acidity) and bitterness (tannin) towards the back of the mouth, it may take a second or two before the sensations of acidity and bitterness occur.

We experience acidity not only as a citric-like taste, but also as a sensation — a tingling freshness on the sides of the cheeks. Bitterness manifests itself as a dry, rough, woody or overly strong tea flavour, and leaves a scratchy feeling on the palate.

TASTES AND FLAVOURS
Sweetness

All wines contain some sweetness even though they may be perceived as quite sour or bitter, thanks to high acidity and the presence of young tannins. High alcohol, although in itself tasteless, can give the impression of sweetness.

Acidity

If you smell a highly acidic wine, you may find that your saliva glands are activated and your mouth begins to water. What causes this response is acidity. That's why a dry white wine (such as Chablis, dry Riesling, Soave, Brut champagne or dry sherry) is such a good aperitif because, by stimulating the saliva glands and gastric juices, it gives you an appetite.

In contrast, a sweet wine before a meal will coat the tongue with sugar and depress your appetite.

In addition to giving you an appetite, a dry wine will also help you digest your meal. The measure of wine's acidity — its pH — is very similar to the pH of our stomach acids.

What are the acids in wine? The main acids in grapes are tartaric, citric and malic. As a product of fermentation, succinic, lactic and acetic acids are formed.

Without acid to give it structure, a wine would have no backbone and would taste flabby. Acid prolongs the taste of the wine and also acts as a preservative while giving the wine its brilliance.

Bitterness — why do young red wines taste bitter?

In young red wines, you will experience a bitter component once the wine has washed over your entire palate. This taste and sensation is *tannin*, a naturally occurring compound in the skins, stalks and pits of grapes. You can taste it in its raw state by biting into the stalks and pits of any grape. The bitter taste also leaves an astringent sensation on the roof and sides of the mouth.

Tannin allows a red wine to age gracefully. Over the years it will soften as the wine reaches its plateau of maturity. Ultimately, it will precipitate out as a dusty sediment in older wines.

There are also tannins in oak barrels which are leached out by the new wine. These are softer than grape tannins. The harder the

grapes are pressed, the more tannin in the wine. Because tannin is so strong a taste, it can mask the fruit in the wine. That is why many red wines have to be aged to allow the tannins to soften and the fruit to express itself both on the nose and on the palate.

A red wine (such as Bordeaux or Burgundy) that has spent a long time macerating on the skins — two weeks or more — will have extracted a lot of tannins and will take several years to become "drinkable."

Most winemakers will destem the grapes during the crush to cut down the amount of tannin when the berries are pressed. Special machines with an auger-like screw separate the berries from the stems and cut the skins at the same time before fermentation.

The lower the amount of tannin in the finished wine, the sooner it will be table-ready.

Oak — why put wine in oak barrels?

Wines that are fermented or aged in oak barrels will extract flavour elements from the wood. There are several different types of oak grown in French forests. The most often used in making barrels are Limousin, Tronçais, Allier, Nevers and Voges. These oaks are more tightly grained and less aromatic than American white oak which is grown in many countries around the world. Each style of oak adds its own unique character to the wine.

Oak barrels, unlike stainless-steel tanks, allow air to come in contact with the wine. Oxygen ages the wine, helps it to mature and soften its tannins.

The flavours of oak are also imparted to the wine. Judicious use of oak can enhance the total effect, although an overly long stay in the barrel will give the wine a predominantly oaky flavour and bouquet. Oak should be used as a chef employs spices — to highlight and enhance the flavour of the wine.

WINE PROFILES

White Wines

VERY DRY, LIGHT	
FRANCE	Aligoté, Crépy, Jura, Muscadet, Petit Chablis, Quincy, Riesling, Saumur, Savoie, Silvaner, Touraine
GERMANY/AUSTRIA	Grüner Veltliner, Riesling Trocken, Silvaner
ITALY	Castelli Romani, Colli Albani, Collio, Est!Est!Est!, Frascati, Galestro, Grüner Veltliner, Marino, Riesling Italico, Riesling Renano, Tocai Friulano,
SPAIN/PORTUGAL	Azietao, Valdepeñas, Vinho Verde
EUROPE	Auxerrois (Luxembourg), Fendant (Swiss), Furmint (Hungary), Riesling (Swiss), Riesling (Hungary), Riesling (Bulgaria), Trakya (Turkey)
CANADA	Aligoté, Auxerrois, Gamay Blanc, Riesling, Seyval
UNITED STATES	Riesling (Washington), Riesling (NY), Seyval (NY)
AUSTRALIA/ NEW ZEALAND	some Rieslings, some Sauvignons

DRY, MEDIUM-BODIED

FRANCE	Beaujolais Blanc, Chablis, Entre-Deux-Mers, Graves, Mâcon Blanc, Pouilly-Fumé, Sancerre, Sauvignon Blanc
GERMANY/AUSTRIA:	Müller-Thurgau, Riesling (QbA), Silvaner (Rheinpfalz), Silvaner (Rheinhessen), Welschriesling
ITALY	Chardonnay, Cortese di Gavi, Lacrima Christi, Orvieto, Pinot Bianco, Pinot Grigio, Soave, Tocai di Lison, Torre di Giano, Traminer, Trebbiano, Verdicchio, Vernaccia di S. Gimignano
SPAIN/PORTUGAL	Bairrada, Chardonnay, Dão whites, Penedes white, Rioja white, Rueda white, Sauvignon, Vina Sol
EUROPE	Chardonnay (Hungary/Bulgaria), Demestica (Greece), Muscat Dry , Sauvignon (Slovenia), Retsina, Sylvaner
CANADA	Chardonnay, Gewürztraminer, Muscat, Pinot Blanc, Vidal, some Riesling
UNITED STATES	Chardonnay (NY), some California Chardonnay, Fumé Blanc, Sauvignon Blanc
AUSTRALIA/ NEW ZEALAND	some Chardonnay, Riesling (NZ), Sauvignon Blanc, Semillon/Chardonnay
SOUTH AMERICA	Chardonnay, Riesling, Sauvignon Blanc
SOUTH AFRICA	Colombar, Steen

DRY, FULL-BODIED	
FRANCE	Chardonnay (South), Condrieu, Côte de Beaune, Gewürztraminer, Pinot Gris, Pouilly-Fuissé (estate), Rhône
GERMANY/AUSTRIA	Baden whites, Muscat, Traminer, Weissburgunder, Grauburgunder
ITALY	Chardonnay (estate), Corvo, Fiano di Avelino, Greco di Tufo, Locorotondo, Regaleali, Torbato, Trebbiano d'Abruzzo
SPAIN/PORTUGAL	Chardonnay (Penedes), Colares, Dão, Garrafeira, Rioja (Murrieta, Muga), Verdejo
EUROPE	Chardonnay, Sauvignon Blanc
CANADA	some Chardonnay
UNITED STATES	Chardonnay (estate), Fumé Blanc (estate), Zinfandel (white)
AUSTRALIA/ NEW ZEALAND	Chardonnay (estate), Marsanne, Muscat, Sauvignon Blanc (estate),
SOUTH AMERICA	some Chardonnay, some Sauvignon Blanc, some Semillon
SOUTH AFRICA	Blanc Fumé, Chardonnay

FRUITY (OFF-DRY), LIGHT TO FULL-BODIED (1) light-bodied (m) medium-bodied (f) full-bodied	
FRANCE	Anjou (l) , Château Chalon (f), Gewürztraminer (late harvest) (f), Edelzwicker (l), Gaillac (l), Jurançon (l), Muscat (m), Pinot Blanc (m), Riesling (late harvest) (f), Sauternes (dry) (f), Savennières (m), Tokay-Pinot Gris (f), Vin jaune (f), Vouvray (f)
GERMANY/AUSTRIA	Grauburgunder, Gewürztraminer, Liebfraumilch, Pinot Blanc (Aus.), Ruländer, Scheurebe, Spätlese, Auslese
ITALY	Frascati Superiore, Malvasia, Müller-Thurgau, Orvieto Classico, Verduzzo
SPAIN/PORTUGAL	Bucelas, Masia Bach, Mateus white
EUROPE	Riesling, Sylvaner, Traminer, Hársleveü (Hungary), Pinot Gris (Hungary), Tokay (dry)
CANADA	Chenin Blanc, Ehrenfelser, late harvest Gewürztraminer, Riesling (BC), Scheurebe, Vidal
UNITED STATES	"Chablis", Gewürztraminer, Riesling, Vignoles/Ravat (NY)
AUSTRALIA/ NEW ZEALAND	some Chardonnay, Chenin Blanc, Riesling, Semillon/Chardonnay
SOUTH AMERICA	Riesling
SOUTH AFRICA	Chenin Blanc (Steen)

SWEET, LIGHT TO FULL-BODIED

FRANCE	Banyuls (f), Barsac (f), Beaumes-de-Venise (f), Cérons (light), Côteaux du Layon (l), Loupiac (m), Rivesaltes (f), Ste-Croix-du-Mont (m), Sauternes (f), Vin de paille (f), Vouvray (m)
GERMANY/AUSTRIA	Beerenauslese (m), Eiswein (m), Trockenbeerenauslese (f)
ITALY	Aleatico (m), Albana di Romagna (m), Malvasia di Lipari (f), Moscato (l), Orvieto Abboccato (l), Passito (f), Picolit (m), Recioto di Soave (f), Verduzzo (m), Vin Santo (f)
SPAIN/PORTUGAL	Granjo (m), Malvasia (m), Muscatel (m), Setubal (f)
EUROPE	Samos Muscat (f), Tokay (f)
CANADA	Icewine (f), Riesling B.A. (m)
UNITED STATES	late harvest Riesling (m), Quady whites, "Sauternes"
AUSTRALIA/ NEW ZEALAND	late harvest Sauvignon (f), late harvest Semillon (f), Muscadel (f), Muscat (f)
SOUTH AFRICA	Edelkeur (f), late harvest Steen (f), late harvest Sauvignon Blanc (f), Muscat (f), Jerepigo

Red Wines

LIGHT-BODIED	
FRANCE	Alsatian Pinot Noir, Anjou Gamay, Beaujolais, Bouzy Rouge, Cassis, Chinon, Clairette, Côtes d'Auvergne, Fronsac, Haut Poitou, Jura, Savoie
GERMANY/AUSTRIA	most reds
ITALY	Bardolino, Freisa, Grignolino, Lago di Caldaro, Lambrusco, Marzemino, Santa Maddelena, Valpolicella
SPAIN/PORTUGAL	Galician reds, Somontano, Vinho Verde
EUROPE	Luxembourg reds, Swiss reds
CANADA	B.C. reds, Chelois, Chambourcin, Gamay, Pinot Noir
UNITED STATES	Claret, Gamay
AUSTRALIA/ NEW ZEALAND	Nouveau wines
SOUTH AFRICA	Gamay
MEDIUM-BODIED	
FRANCE	Beaujolais villages, Bordeaux (non-vintate), Bourgueil, Burgundy villages, Corbières, Côtes de Bergerac, Gaillac, Loire Cabernet

GERMANY/AUSTRIA	Auslese reds, Dornfelder
ITALY	Barbera, Bonarda, Cabernet, Carema, Chianti, Castelli Romani, Dolcetto, Ghemme, Pinot Nero, Regaleali, Sangiovese, Valtellina
EUROPE	Demestica, Nemea, Kratosija, Merlot, Pinot Noir
CANADA	Baco Noir, Cabernet Franc, Cabernet Sauvignon, Marechal Foch, Merlot
UNITED STATES	Barbera, East Coast reds, Oregon Pinot Noir
AUSTRALIA/ New Zealand	"Burgundy", Pinot Noir, Merlot
SOUTH AMERICA	Argentinian reds, Pinot Noir, Uruguayan reds
SOUTH AFRICA	Pinot Noir, Merlot

FULL-BODIED:

FRANCE	Bandol, Bergerac, Bordeaux (château-bottled), Burgundy (domaine-bottled), Cahors, Châteauneuf-du-Pape, Côtes du Ventoux, Fitou, Lirac, Pécharmant, Provence, Rhône
GERMANY/AUSTRIA	barrel-aged Cabernet
ITALY	Barbaresco, Barolo, Cannonau, Carmignano , Chianti Classico Riserva, Gattinara, Nebbiolo d'Alba, Montepulcianio d'Abbruzzo, Refosco, Rubesco, Sassicaia,

	Sfursat, Spanna, Taurasi, Tignanello, Vino Nobile
SPAIN/PORTUGAL	Bairrada, Colares, Dão, Navarra, Penedes, Rioja
EUROPE	Bulgarian reds, Château Musar (Lebanon), Greek reds, Hungarian reds
CANADA	some Cabernet Sauvignon/Merlot
UNITED STATES	Cabernet Sauvignon, Merlot, Petite Syrah, Zinfandel
AUSTRALIA/ NEW ZEALAND	Cabernet, Shiraz (Hermitage)
SOUTH AMERICA	Chilean Cabernet
SOUTH AFRICA	Cabernet, Merlot, Pinotage, Roodeberg
HEAVY-DUTY	
FRANCE	Côte Rôtie, Hermitage
ITALY	Amarone, Brunello di Montalcino, Castel del Monte
SPAIN/PORTUGAL	Garrafeiras
EUROPE	Bull's Blood (Egri Bikaver), Kasteler, Postup
UNITED STATES	some Cabernets, some Petite Sirahs, some Zinfandel

AUSTRALIA/ NEW ZEALAND	some Cabernet/Shiraz, some Shiraz (Hermitage)
SOUTH AMERICA	some Cabernets, some Merlots
SOUTH AFRICA	some Cabernet blends
SWEET REDS	
FRANCE	Banyuls, Rasteau
ITALY	Giro, Recioto della Valpolicella
EUROPE	Mavrodaphne, Port (Portugal)
UNITED STATES	Port, Quady reds
AUSTRALIA/ NEW ZEALAND	Port
SOUTH AMERICA	Port
SOUTH AFRICA	Port, Jerepigo, Red Muscat

Tannic Wines Need Time

The following red grapes and the wine styles made from them are likely to be tannic when young. They will taste astringent and bitter on the finish. This will register on the roof of your mouth and on the cheeks and gums. These wines will need a few years in the bottle to soften up.

Cabernet Sauvignon - red Bordeaux

Merlot - St. Emilion, Pomerol

Pinot Noir - red Burgundy

Syrah - Crozes-Hermitage, Hermitage, Côte Rôtie

Shiraz - Hermitage (Australia)

Aglianico - Taurasi

Nebbiolo - Barolo, Barbaresco

Sangiovese - Chianti, Brunello di Montalcino, Vino Nobile di Montepulciano

Tempranillo - red Rioja, Navarra and Penedes (Spain)

Zinfandel - Zinfandel

Oaky Wines

The following wines are likely to smell and taste oaky.

Australia: Chardonnay, Cabernet Sauvignon, Shiraz

California: Chardonnay, Cabernet Sauvignon, Merlot, Zinfandel

Spain: Rioja, Navarra, Penedes, Ribero del Duero

Portuguese garrafeiras

South American reds

New Zealand reds

Italian Barolos and Babarescos

Eastern European reds

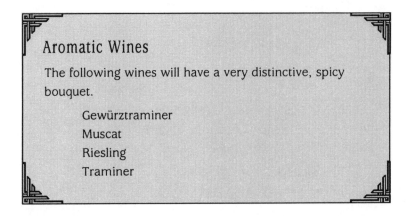

Aromatic Wines

The following wines will have a very distinctive, spicy bouquet.

Gewürztraminer
Muscat
Riesling
Traminer

Wine Trivia

By using different winemaking techniques on red grapes, you can make a white wine, a rosé, a light-bodied or a full-bodied red wine depending on how long you leave the skins and pulp of the grapes in contact with their juice.

SPARKLING WINES

First, let's define our terms. Champagne is sparkling wine, but there are very few sparkling wines that are champagne. While Canadians — and North and South Americans in general — have yet to acknowledge that champagne only comes from the Champagne district of France, European wine regions respect the convention.

The Spanish call their sparkling wine *cava*. The Germans call theirs *Sekt*, and the Italians, who have yet to make a final decision on the matter, call theirs *classimo* or *metodo classico*. In South Africa, it's *Cap Classique*. Even French sparkling wines made in Alsace, Burgundy, Loire, Jura and Savoie, Rhône and Southwest France cannot be called "champagne," and outside of the Champagne region the term *vin mousseux* (sparkling wine) is employed.

There are basically three ways to make a wine sparkle.

- **The Champagne Method**: You make a still wine and then give it a second fermentation in the bottle by adding a little sugar and yeast. The action of the yeast converts the sugar to alcohol and carbon dioxide is produced as a by-product. The closed bottle ensures that the gas has nowhere to go and gets bound into the wine. Since it is a very labour-intensive process, the product is expensive. It goes without saying that the quality is superior to sparkling wines made by other means.

- **The Charmat Method**: This process is a way to make sparkling wines in bulk. Developed by a French wine-scientist named Eugene Charmat in 1910, this process is much less expensive and time-consuming than the champagne method, but the quality is inferior (and the bubbles are bigger). The principle is similar to the champagne method except that the secondary fermentation takes place in a large, sealed tank rather than a bottle. The finished wine is drawn off under pressure and then bottled.

- **The "Bicycle Pump" Method**: The product is injected with carbon dioxide in tank or on the bottling line before the closure is pushed home. This process is used for inexpensive pop wines. The bubbles last for about as long as it takes to consume a glass.

Spanish *cavas* are made by the champagne method, but they are much less expensive than French champagne. The costs of making cavas are much lower because the Spanish have developed machines to do the elaborate work of "cleaning up" the wine. In France, this part of the process — which involves shaking and tilting each bottle until the dead yeast cells settle on the cork — is called *remouage*, and it takes several weeks of movements by hand of highly skilled operators.

No beverage is as cruel as champagne or sparkling wine when it comes to showing up how clean your glasses are. Any dirt will cause the bubbles to cling to the side of the glass. Dishwasher film will have the same effect. Instead of tiny bubbles rising upwards in a continuous flow, fat lazy bubbles hug the side of the glass, clinging to the dirt. Be sure to have the glasses wiped with clean, lint-free towels or paper.

Any wetness in the glass will also cause problems. Water will kill the bubbles, so don't wet the glasses and put them in the freezer for that chilled, frosted look. Not only will this turn the wine flat when it hits the icy sides of the glass, but it will bring down the temperature to a point where tasting is all but impossible. Any sparkling wine to be at the right serving temperature needs only 20 to 30 minutes in an ice bucket that has been half-filled with ice cubes and water.

Opening Champagne

The pressure inside a bottle of champagne is 90 pounds per square inch. If the bottle is warmed up or shaken, this pressure is increased. Once the wire muzzle under the foil has been removed, you have in your hand a live grenade with the pin removed.

A champagne cork, if left to its own devices, will eject from the bottle at a speed approaching 65 km per hour. So always keep your thumb over the cork until you remove it.

The way trained sommeliers open sparkling wine bottles so that there is no "pop" followed by an explosion of wine is to hold the cork in a stable fashion in one hand while gently twisting the bottle away from it in the other. Have a cloth handy in case the wine does bubble over, and make sure that the glasses are within easy reach so that you can pour immediately.

The bubbles in champagne and sparkling wines rise quickly in the glass and then settle back to the level of the liquid, so pour one-third of a glass and wait until the bubbles subside before pouring the rest.

Champagne Glasses

The worst glass for champagne is the one you see most frequently in movies: the one shaped like a saucer or ice-cream coupe. This shape will ensure that the wine warms up quickly (because of the large surface area) and will lose its sparkle. When you take a sip you're in danger of giving your nose a bath. Legend has it that the coupe glass was designed for Queen Victoria who reacted badly to the gassiness of champagne. The glass was engineered to take the bubbles out of the wine as quickly as possible.

The best-shaped glass for all sparkling wines is a slender tulip or flute with enough of a stem so that your hand does not touch the bowl. The heat of your skin will warm up the wine and you will mask the inspiring sight of the bubbles rising.

THE IDEAL TASTING GLASS

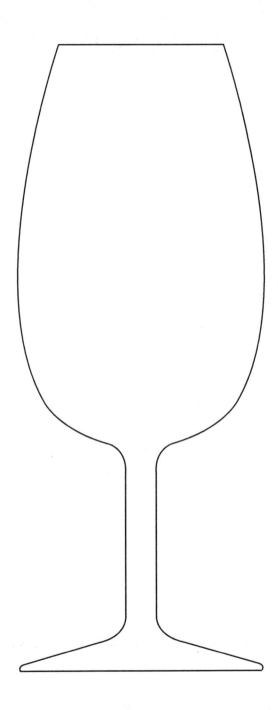

CHAPTER 4

Wine and Health

*E*ven those who have never had a drink of wine, spirits or beer have alcohol present in their systems. Bacterial activity in the body breaks down sugars and starches and converts them to alcohol at a rate of about one ounce a day.

We also consume alcohol in fruit juices and medicines, and we break them down in our systems the same way we break down alcohol in wine. Most people will metabolize alcohol at the rate of 10 mL per hour — that's 10 mL of absolute alcohol, not 10 mL of wine, beer or spirits.

If you drink wine on an empty stomach, alcohol will be absorbed into your bloodstream much faster than if you drink the wine with food. Always have food when you drink.

THE BENEFITS OF WINE

The modest consumption of wine does have salubrious effects:
* helps rid the blood of low density lipoproteins (fatty substances in cholesterol that clog the arteries)
* aids digestion (the pH of wine is similar to the pH of our stomach acid)

- stimulates the appetite
- helps reduce stress
- acts as a diuretic
- acts as a (non-chemical) sedative and tranquilizer
- acts as a morale booster for the aged and recuperating patients
- can cut down susceptibility to the common cold
- appears to lower the risk of certain types of cancers (although it can cause breast cancer)
- provides a stimulant to good conversation
- promotes a convivial atmosphere

Wine and Your Heart

Clinical studies have shown that a moderate intake of wine can lower the risk of heart disease. The question now is, What is a moderate amount? Most doctors suggest two 5-ounce glasses a day.

WARNING LABELS

Wines sold in the United States have labels that read "Contains Sulphites." This is to alert individuals who suffer allergies to sulfites. Sulphur dioxide is produced naturally by yeasts during fermentation which means that every bottle of wine will contain sulphites even if the winemaker has not added sulphur products during the vinting process.

Sulfites are widely used in salad bars and by producers of dried fruits, but in neither case are these producers required to post warning labels. Sulphur, in various forms, is used in the wine-making process as an anti-oxidant and an anti-bacterial agent. Just as our bodies produce alcohol so do they make sulfites, enough in a 24-hour-hour period equivalent to the sulfite content of 100 bottles of wine!

Sulphites are compounds of sulphur formed in wine when sulphur dioxide in liquid form or a sulphite-bearing agent such as potassium metabisulphite is added to prevent the wine from oxidizing or spoiling because of bacterial acitivity.

Sulphur is also extensively used to rid barrels of bacteria. Sulphur candles are burned inside to fumigate them.

FETAL ALCOHOL SYNDROME

In certain provinces, notices are displayed in restaurants and bars with the unequivocal message that alcohol can harm the unborn baby. According to Dr. Ernest Abel, Director of the Mott Center for Human Growth and Development in Detroit, Michigan, pregnant women don't need to be concerned about Fetal Alcohol Syndrome if they take one drink a week.

The *British Medical Journal* (Vol. 303, 1991) reported on a study of nearly six hundred 18-month-old children in Dundee, Scotland: "Pregnant women probably need not abstain from alcohol altogether as no detectable adverse relation was found between the child's mental and physical development and the mother's weekly consumption at levels in excess of 100 grams absolute alcohol (10 drinks per week). . . . The children of mothers who had reduced their intake did not differ from those abstainers, suggesting that consumption of at least 350 grams absolute alcohol (35 drinks) a week throughout pregnancy is required to influence mental and physical development."

Wine Additives

Apart from sulphur products used to prevent oxidation and spoilage, the only other compounds added to wine are:

- Sugar (to boost alcohol when necessary)
- Tartaric acid (the natural acid of grapes, to adjust acid levels)
- Fining agents to take out the tiny particles and render the wine crystal clear

The most commonly used fining agents are:

- Bentonite — a highly purefied diatomaceous earth
- Gelatin — what you find in Jello
- Caseinate — casein is one of the chief constituents of milk

These fining agents when poured into a vat, tank or barrel of wine coagulate and draw the tiny particles in suspension together by an electrical charge and cause them to fall to the bottom. Once the wine is racked off to another container, it is bright and clear.

Traditionally, fining materials were egg whites (still used in the best Bordeaux châteaux and by some California producers); fresh (or dried) ox blood; isinglass (a very pure form of gelatin found in sturgeon bladders).

CHAPTER 5

How to Talk Winespeak

*T*here is a vocabulary of wine that experts use among themselves to describe the bouquet, taste, style and health of a wine. You may come across some of these terms in restaurants where enterprising sommeliers add descriptions of the wines on their wine list. Or they may crop up on shelf-talkers and other promotional blurbs at your local liquor store. Don't be put off by the jargon; it's really only a shorthand way of describing wine.

Acidic: Usually a thumbs-down term, meaning the wine is overly acidic and therefore tastes sharp like lemon juice.

Aftertaste: When you swallow the wine, you are left with a residual taste that can stay in the mouth for a significant amount of time. The mark of a great wine is how long the taste remains. By the same token, the aftertaste of a wine can be poor if it is tannic or overly acidic.

Alcoholic: An alcoholic wine is one that feels heavy in the mouth and hot as it goes down your throat. You can tell that a wine is high in alcohol if you swirl the glass and the transparent film of liquid left on the side of the glass is thick and slow moving as it falls back to the surface of the wine.

Aroma: Basically, the smell of the grapes in freshly made wine. In other words, the recognizable perfume of a specific grape variety. Bouquet, on the other hand, is the smell of wine that has aged in the bottle and has become more complex. A mature wine (one that has aged for 15 years or more) may give off a bouquet that has nothing to do with fruits, flowers or vegetables. It can can a mixture of more organic smells such as leather, chocolate and coffee beans.

Aromatic: Think of a rich, spicy perfume that pervades the taste of the wine as well as its bouquet. Good examples are Gewürztraminer and Muscat.

Astringent: This has more to do with a tactile sensation than a taste. A wine that is high in tannin and acidity will leave a dry, scratchy feeling on the roof of the mouth and sides of the cheeks. Young red Bordeaux or Barolo can be very astringent.

Austere: This is a polite term for a wine that's really hard to drink because it lacks fruit and any other pleasurable qualities. Usually applied to expensive wines that should taste better, but because you've paid a bundle for them, you don't want to admit that you bought a dog. The opposite is *generous*.

Backward: A wine that should have developed but hasn't. Slow to mature. Needs more time in the cellar.

Baked: Grapes grown in hot climates can get "sun-burnt," especially if there is little rainfall. This can give the wines a baked character. You can taste a roasted, earthy flavour in the wines.

Balance: A wine is in balance when all of its components — fruit, alcohol, acidity, tannin and oak — are harmonious. If one or more of these parts predominates, the wine will be out of balance.

Barnyard: A bouquet most characteristic of some red and white Burgundies (and Pinot Noirs and Chardonnays grown in other regions). If you have ever mucked out a stable you will know this smell — slightly rotting hay with an overtone of manure. Sounds revolting, but in a wine it has an attractive quality and is a term of praise. (Wine people are weird!)

Beaujolais Nouveau: A wine to drink young, lightly chilled. The new wine is released on the third Thursday in November. (see **Carbonic Maceration**)

Bitter: A taste that can result from tannin (bite into a grape pit and see how bitter it is) or from underripe grapes or the grapes from young vines.

Blush: A style of wine made usually from Zinfandel in California. The colour has a faint tinge of pink and a perceptible sweetness. Produced in the same way as rosé — a few hours of skin contact with the juice to extract a little colour. (See **Rosé**)

Body: A wine is either light-bodied, medium-bodied or full-bodied. This is a direct result of the amount of alcohol in the wine and the extract from the grape. Body expresses itself as weight in the mouth.

Botrytis: A disease whose full Latin name is *Botrytis cinerea* that attacks the skins of ripened grapes in warm, humid conditions. This fungus-like growth pierces the skins and allows the water to evaporate thus concentrating the sugars and the acids. The dried-out grapes look disgusting on the vine (rather like dead bats in an anatomy class) but they make wonderfully honeyed wines such as Sauternes and Beerenauslese wines. Botrytis has a characteristic smell of petrol and honey.

Bottle-Age: Wines, unlike spirits, mature in glass bottles. They change over the years whereas scotch or gin remain the same. Bottle-age gives wine a mellowness over the years and a more intense bouquet. Eventually, a wine that has matured will begin to decline.

Bottle-Sickness: There will be a great difference of taste between a wine in the cask and one that has been newly bottled. The act of bottling introduces large quantities of oxygen into the wine that initially produces untrue flavours before the wine settles down after a few weeks.

Bouquet: The smell of a wine when you pull the cork and pour some into a glass. With practice, you can tell the condition of the wine as well as its taste from this smell. That's why wine waiters give you a sample in your glass before pouring for the whole table. (see **Aroma**)

Buttery: A smell and a taste usually associated with oak-aged Chardonnay grown in warm climates such as California and Australia.

Carbonic Maceration: A technique first used in Beaujolais to make light fruity red wines that can be consumed young. Whole uncrushed grape clusters are placed in a closed stainless-steel vat. The top grapes because of their weight eventually press down on those at the bottom, breaking their skins and starting a fermentation. The fermentation jumps in a chain reaction to each of the individual berries and occurs inside the skins. Very little tannin is extracted this way and when the grapes are lightly pressed after a few days the wine can be consumed within a matter of weeks. This is how Beaujolais Nouveau is made.

Cat's Pee: A smell associated with Sauvignon Blanc wines, usually when the grapes get overripe. Self-explanatory.

Cedar: A smell of fine red Bordeaux wines, associated with the Cabernet Sauvignon grape. Sometimes called "cigar box."

Chocolate: A smell you can find in rich red wines, especially from the Rhône.

Clean: Devoid of flaws, off-odours and unpleasant tastes.

Complex: A wine that has many levels of perfumes and taste sensations. In other words, an interesting and very good wine.

Corked: A wine that has turned — usually because of oxidation — and smells and tastes of vinegar. It may have a brown hue to its colour in both whites and reds. It has nothing to do with the cork. (see **Corky**)

Corky: The smell of a bad cork in the wine. A cork that is infected can change the taste of the wine, or traces of the bleaching agent used to whiten it can add a chemical flavour.

Creamy: A sensation of the wine on the palate. An unctuous fruitiness and softness found in Chardonnays grown in warm conditions.

Crisp: A description of white wines with perceptible acidity. Wines that refresh the palate.

Depth: A wine that has different levels of enjoyment; a richness of bouquet and flavour that changes in the glass.

Dry: A wine whose sugars have been fully fermented. There will be some residual sweetness from the fruit, but the acidity will give it a dry finish.

Dumb: A wine that has nothing to say. An undeveloped, immature wine whose bouquet and flavours are locked in. The oenological equivalent of a taciturn adolescent.

Dusty: The aftertaste and mouthfeel of maturing tannins in red wines.

Earthy: Tasting of the soil; a quality found in reds from hot growing regions.

Elegant: A well-balanced wine of high quality. This term is used mainly when describing lighter wines. Rich, full-bodied wines would be termed robust or meaty, or some other graphic term.

Eucalyptus: Certain Californian and Australian Cabernet Sauvignons have a bouquet of eucalyptus because the grapes are overripe. This can also manifest itself as a bell pepper smell.

Extract: Soluble solids from pressed grapes (other than its sugars) that give the wine body and weight.

Fat: A weight-challenged wine, full of alcohol and extract, heavy on the palate. Overly rich. Can be a compliment or a criticism, depending on context.

Finesse: A synonym for elegance. A wine whose elements are in perfect harmony.

Finish: The final taste of the wine. The sensory impression left in the mouth once you have swallowed it.

Firm: A wine that has structure (thanks to its acidity) as opposed to flabby. (see **Flabby**)

First Growth: This does not refer to anything that happens in the vineyard. It is, in fact, a designation of quality for Bordeaux wines. In 1855, the wines of the Médoc and Graves were divided by price and quality into five growths (*crus*). The First Growths were the top wines.

Flabby: A wine that lacks acidity to give it structure and length of finish. Such a wine will taste sweet and soft on the palate and go nowhere.

Flat: A wine that lies on the palate and bores you to death. No flavour, no life in it. Also refers to a sparkling wine that has been left too long in the glass and all the bubbles have disappeared.

Flinty: Certain cold-climate wines, such as Sauvignon Blanc, can have a bouquet reminiscent of struck flint, slightly smoky.

Floral: Smelling of flowers. You find flower smells in Riesling (spring flowers), Gewürztraminer (roses) and some reds (lilac, iris).

Forward: A young wine that is showing more maturity than its age suggests. An over-achiever.

Foxy: The smell of wines made from labrusca grapes (the native North American varieties such as Concord and Niagara). An unpleasant aroma that puts you in mind of a dog that's been left out in the rain. The term derives from wild or "fox" grapes.

Fresh: A wine whose bouquet starts your mouth watering and whose taste enlivens and cleanses the palate because of its crisp acidity.

Fruity: A wine with good extract that tastes of fruit — cherries, plums, gooseberry, melon, blackberries, blackcurrants, etc.

Full-Bodied: A high-alcohol wine that feels rich and weighty in the mouth.

Geranium: One flower you do not want to smell in a wine. Its unpleasant odour indicates a microbiological fault in the wine induced during fermentation.

Grapey: Certain wines taste exactly like the fresh grapes they were made from — Muscat and Muscatelle are prime examples.

Green: Wines that taste immature either because the grapes were not ripe enough at harvest or the vines are still young.

Grip: A wine with a real presence that asserts itself on the palate and has grip.

Hard: A wine that has excessive tannin that will take several years of bottle-aging to soften up. Examples: Barolo, red Bordeaux.

Herbaceous: Smelling of freshly cut grass and flowers. A term often applied to young white wines, particularly Sauvignon Blanc.

Honeyed: Sweet wines take on a honey-like bouquet with age. You can smell honey in Sauternes, old late harvest Rieslings and Icewines.

Lees: A heavy sediment of grape particles thrown by young wines in barrel or tank. If a wine is left on the lees (*sur lie* in French), it will develop more flavour.

Legs: When a glass is swirled, the alcohol clings to the sides of the glass and eventually falls back to the surface of the wine in tears or "legs." The Germans call this phenomenon "church windows," which these legs resemble. The thickness of the legs and the speed at which they move gives you an indication of the wine's alcoholic strength. The slower, the higher the alcohol content.

Length: The staying power of a wine's aftertaste. The longer you can taste it, the better the wine.

Light: Lacking body (alcohol), but not necessarily flavour. The wines of the Mosel in Germany are light but have wonderfully rich Riesling flavours.

Luscious: A term used to describe dessert wines when the sweetness, creaminess and softness are balanced with enough acidity not to let the wine cloy on the palate.

Maderised: Comes from the word "Madeira." Whites wines, when they get too old, begin to turn brown and taste like bad Madeira — slightly oxidized, flat and tinny.

Medium-Dry: A wine that has perceptible sweetness, but finishes dry. Examples are some Vouvray, Chenin Blanc, Riesling Spätlese.

Medium-Sweet: One level above Medium-Dry on the sweetness scale. Examples: Riesling Auslese, Picolit.

Must: The juice of white grapes or the juice and skins of black grapes before fermentation.

Musty: The smell of a dank cellar usually associated with a bad cork or a dirty barrel.

Noble Rot: An easier name for the benign disease *Botrytis cinerea*. (see above)

Nose: The smell of a wine; its bouquet or aroma.

Oaky: The smell and the taste of oak in a wine, especially apparent when the oak is new. The smells and flavours can range from vanilla and coconut to spices such as nutmeg, cinnamon and cloves.

Off-Dry: A wine that has some residual sweetness, but finishes dry. Examples: German Rieslings, most white house blends.

Oxydized: A wine that has been exposed to air, rendering it flat and prune-like in taste.

Petrol: Yes, gasoline. The characteristic smell of aging Riesling— and very appealing, too.

Pétillant (French): Slightly sparkling, but not visibly so. A sensation of bubbles on the tongue.

Plonk: A humorous description of a simple, every-day quaffing wine.

Racy: A fresh, light white wine with stimulating acidity. Examples: Mosel Riesling, Vinho Verde, Fendant.

Rosé: A pink wine either dry or semi-sweet made from red grapes. The newly pressed grape juice is left in contact with the skins for a matter of hours to extract the colour desired by the winemaker.

Short: A wine whose flavour suddenly drops out. A wine with no discernible finish, usually as a result of rains during the harvest that swell the grapes and consequently dilute the fruit and sugars.

Soft: A wine that has mellowed with age. Sweet wines will also have a softness because the sugar will mask the acidity.

Spicy: Exotic spiciness like cardamom, found particularly in Gewürztraminer.

Spritzig (German): A prickling on the tongue from wines that have bound-in carbon dioxide. (see **Pétillant**)

Stemmy: A green, bitter taste of grape stems causing excess tannin in the wine.

Sulphur: Sulphur and sulphur compounds are used to prevent oxidation and to kill off any bacteria in wine. In France, barrels are cleaned by burning sulphur sticks inside them.

Sulphury: The smell of sulphur in wine that has been overly treated with sulphur products. Up to 30 parts per million sulphur is barely detectable on the nose. More than this and you get a burnt match-head smell.

Tannin: An astringent, bitter-tasting compound that occurs naturally in the skins, stalks and pits of grapes. Wood tannins are present in oak barrels, too. Tannin acts as a preservative, allowing a red wine to age gracefully. Eventually, the tannin will precipitate out and fall to the bottom of the bottle as a fine sediment.

Tart: A wine that is high in acidity, usually because of unripe grapes.

Vanilla: The smell and taste of new oak, especially evident in Australian wines.

Varietal: A single grape type whose name will appear on the label in New World wines. Examples: Chardonnay, Merlot, Pinot Gris.

Vinegar: If a wine smells of vinegar, send it back. It's over the hill.

Volatile Acidity: Too much and the wine begins to smell and taste like balsamic vinegar. All wines contain some, but in excessive amounts it shows that the wine is starting to become vinegar.

Weight: How the wine feels in the mouth. The heavier on the palate, the more alcohol. Weightier wines come from the hotter growing regions where sunshine can build up grape sugars.

Woody: A wine that has been kept too long in oak, imparting a woody flavour.

Yeasty: The smell of fermentation in young wines; a kind of bready aroma.

Caudalie: The Unit of On-Going Pleasure

The French, bless them, have come up with a way of measuring a sensory perception — the aftertaste of a wine. The better the wine the longer the flavour will linger in the mouth. Their basic unit, a *caudalie*, is the number of seconds that a given wine will leave its impression on the palate after you have swallowed it.

CHAPTER 6

The Anatomy of Drinking Wine

*O*ne of the most often-asked questions about wine is "When should a given wine be opened?" The implication is that there is a time when wine is at its best. If opened too soon, it may be harsh or unbalanced. If opened too late, it may taste "off."

It may come as a surprise, but a good 90 percent of wines made around the world today are not for laying down. They are meant to be enjoyed as soon as you buy them. In some cases, the fresher the wine, the better it will be. *This is particularly true of most white wines and sparkling wines — even champagne.* Drink them within two years of their vintage date; otherwise, they will begin to taste flat.

Blended table wines with brand names should also be consumed when young. There is little point in laying them down because they won't improve significantly in the bottle. Most of them have been pasteurized (like milk) to kill off any bacteria or cold stabilized (to get rid of tartrates). Pasteurization prolongs their shelf life, but it doesn't allow them to develop in the bottle.

General rule of thumb: If the bottle has a screwcap, do not keep it too long.

WHEN DO I DRINK IT?

Wines for Immediate Consumption

- Most dry white wines *except* barrel-fermented or barrel-aged Chardonnays (white Burgundies), and château-bottled white Bordeaux

- Champagne

- Wines with fantasy names (i.e., Lion Blanc)

- Rosé wines

- Wines without a vintage date

- Beaujolais, Valpolicella and other light reds

- dry sherry

Buy them, bring them home, chill them and pull the cork or undo the cap.

Wines that Need Aging

- red Bordeaux

- red Burgundy

- Rhône reds

- Chianti (Brunello, Vino Nobile)

- Barolo/Barbaresco

- Spanish reds

- Portuguese reds

- Californian Cabernet/Merlot

- Chilean reds

Wines Labelled by Grape Varieties that Improve with Aging
Whites

- Oak-aged or barrel-fermented Chardonnay
- German Riesling
- white Bordeaux
- white Rhône
- Alsatian Tokay-Pinot Gris

Reds

- Cabernet Sauvignon
- Merlot
- Cabernet Franc
- Pinot Noir
- Syrah/Shiraz
- Zinfandel
- Petite Sirah

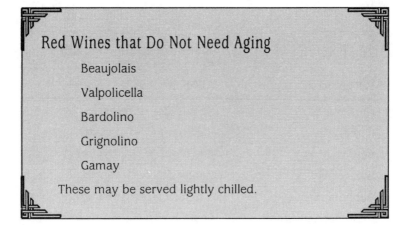

Red Wines that Do Not Need Aging

Beaujolais

Valpolicella

Bardolino

Grignolino

Gamay

These may be served lightly chilled.

How much aging does a wine need?

The degree of aging a wine receives depends on the quality of the finished wine and the grape variety. Certain grapes, such as Cabernet Sauvignon, Nebbiolo and Sangiovese, are high in tannin and need more time in the bottle to soften up. The better the wine, the more time it will need in the bottle. Here is an example.

Let's take four wines of varying price ranges from Bordeaux, beginning with a simple blend:

- Sichel Bordeaux Rouge (a Bordeaux blend): 1 to 3 years (depending on the vintage)

- Calvet St. Emilion (a commune wine): 2 to 5 years

- Château Montlabert (a single estate wine): 3 to 6 years

- Château Lafite (a First Growth wine): 7 to 15 years

The simple Bordeaux Rouge blend is made to be table ready. You can drink it with pleasure as soon as you buy it, but it will improve if you let it age for a year or two. The St. Emilion will prove to be a little tannic if you open it right away, as will the Château Montlabert. It would be most regrettable to open a young Château Lafite but then the price would probably inhibit you, anyway.

Aging Potential of Wines (depending on the vintage)

WINE	REGION
Amarone	Veneto (6 – 15 years)
Barbaresco	Piedmont (5 – 12 years)
Barolo	Piedmont (6 – 20 years)
Beaujolais	Burgundy (1 – 5 years)
Cabernet Sauvignon	Australia (4 – 15 years)
Cabernet Sauvignon	South Africa (5 – 15 years)
Cabernet Sauvignon	California (4 – 15 years)
Cabernet Sauvignon	Chile (3 – 8 years)

Châteauneuf–du–Pâpe	Rhône (5 – 20 years)
Chianti Classico Riserva	Tuscany (4 – 10 years)
Côte de Beaune	Burgundy red (5 – 10 years)
	white (3 – 8 years)
Côte de Nuits	Burgundy red (6 – 15 years)
Côte-Rôtie	Rhône (5 – 20 years)
Médoc/Graves (château-bottled)	Bordeaux (7 – 20 years)
St. Emilion/Pomerol (château-bottled)	Bordeaux (6 – 15 years)
Merlot	California (4 – 8 years)
Rioja Reservas	Spain (7 – 15 years)
Shiraz	Australia (4 – 20 years)

If I want to keep wine for years, how do I do it?

Say the words "wine cellar" and the immediate image conjured up is a dark, damp cave full of ancient bottles, covered with cobwebs, somewhere in the bowels of the earth under a French château or English country house. But these days most cellars are above ground in climate-controlled rooms that keep the bottles at a constant temperature and at the right degree of humidity.

You don't have to have a cellar to store wines. You just need a place that is cool enough and dark enough to allow your bottles to slumber and mature in peace.

CREATING YOUR OWN WINE CELLAR

Putting a cellar in a basement or an upstairs closet is easier than you think.

Having your own cellar will allow you to keep a stock of wines on hand for all occasions and you can watch them grow in value as they mature (10 percent or more a year for the better wines). A

cellar will also enable you to buy young wines at reasonable prices and hold them for years until they are ready for drinking.

Keeping wines over the long haul, whether it be 4,000 bottles in the basement or two dozen in a bedroom closet, requires certain storage conditions. Wines spoil if subjected to excessive heat, light, vibration (proximity to washing machines, fridges, compressors, etc.) and smells (paints, solvents). Wines age best in cool, dark, slightly damp enviroments with good air circulation.

Here are the basic rules when it comes to wine storage:

1. Always lay your bottles so that the corks remain wet at all times. If the bottles are stored vertically, the corks will dry out and air will get in and turn the wine to vinegar.

2. The optimum storage temperatures are between 10 and 13 degrees Celsius, without dramatic fluctuations.

3. Choose a north-facing wall to avoid heat in summer.

4. Ensure some humidity and fresh air circulation.

5. Don't store wines in the kitchen (especially above a fridge) where temperatures constantly rise and fall.

To create a cellar in your basement, monitor temperatures with a thermometer to find the best location. Wall off a section using good insulation, particularly on the ceiling. (Be generous with the allotted space; otherwise, you'll find in two years you've bought three or four times the capacity of your cellar.)

If the ambient temperature remains constant (around 11 or 12 degrees Celsius), you will not need a cooling unit, but one will be necessary if the mercury rises significantly in summer. If the basement is very dry, spread gravel (or small stones) on the cellar floor and water it occasionally.

Install metal or wooden racks (not made of pine or cedar which smell) or construction tiles. If you build the racks yourself, make sure the angle of the bottle keeps wine in contact with the total surface area of the cork. Do not paint or varnish wooden racks.

If you buy your wines in case lots, have honeycomb shelving built so that each diamond shape will accommodate a dozen bot-

tles. Otherwise, choose a single-bottle racking system so you can keep track of your wines more easily.

To convert a walk-in closet in an apartment to a small cellar, insulate the walls and ceiling and install a small air-conditioning unit that is vented to the exterior of the building or into a hall. Place a large bowl of water on the floor to ensure humidity.

Once your cellar is in place, store white wines nearest the floor — the coolest part — and those reds you want to hold for a long time. Wines for current consumption should be stored at the top.

Once finished, your home wine cellar will become quite a topic of conversation. *It may even become your favourite room!*

Now that I have a cellar, what do I put in it?

The wines that you buy will depend upon how you will use them. For instance, do you want to lay down young wines to mature over the years?

One thing I have found through bitter experience is that the size of your cellar, however large it starts out, is never large enough. Once you start collecting wine (a good rule is to buy two bottles for every one you drink), the space begins to fill up remarkably quickly. So, make sure the space you set aside is four or five times the area you think you will need!

A 24-Bottle Sampler Cellar
Reds (one bottle of each)

Bordeaux (château-bottled)

Burgundy (Côte de Beaune or Côte de Nuits)

Rhône (Châteauneuf-du-Pape or Côtes du Rhône)

Beaujolais (Morgon, Fleurie, Moulin-à-Vent, etc.)

California Zinfandel

Oregon Pinot Noir

Chianti Classico Riserva

Valpolicella or Dolcetto

Rioja (Spain)

Dao or Bairrada (Portugal)

Australian Shiraz or Shiraz/Cabernet

South African Pinotage

Chilean Cabernet Sauvignon

Canadian Gamay or Cabernet Franc

Whites (one bottle of each)

Burgundy (Mâcon or Pouilly-Fuissé)

Sancerre or Pouilly Fumé

Bordeaux (Graves or Entre-Deux-Mers)

Alsatian Tokay-Pinot Gris

Alsatian Gewürztraminer

Rheingau Riesling

Californian Fumé Blanc

Australian Chardonnay

Chilean Chardonnay or Sauvignon Blanc

Ontario Chardonnay or Riesling

This Sampler Cellar will allow you to taste wines from the major wine-growing areas of the world and help you to decide your preferences for future stocking.

Having tasted your Sampler Cellar, expand your horizons with more esoteric wines, such as:

Reds

Chinon or Bourgeuil (Loire)

Barolo or Barbaresco (Piedmont)

Vino Nobile di Montepulciano or Brunello di Montalcino (Tuscany)

Greek reds

Cahors (S.W. France)

Portuguese reds

South African Cabernet Sauvignon

Argentinian reds

Ribero del Duero (Spain)

Whites

Rhône

Rioja (Spain)

Vinho Verde (Portugal)

Orvieto (Italy)

Viognier (Rhône, California)

Vouvray (Loire)

Chardonnay (South Africa)

Muscat (Alsace)

Fendant (Switzerland)

Sauternes (Bordeaux)

Late harvest Riesling (California or Germany)

If it is your intention to create a cellar for long-term aging, make sure you balance the contents so that they reach maturity at different times. You don't want to find yourself in the position of waiting six or seven years only to have every bottle ready at the same time. Consult the aging chart on page 62 for the lifespan of different wines.

Always lay down at least two bottles of each wine for aging. You may find you have opened one bottle too soon. Three bottles is the best number if you are not buying in case lots. You can test the maturity when you pull the cork of the first bottle, confirm it when you open the second, and really enjoy the third!

What's a good year?

First let me answer the question, "What is a bad year?" A bad year occurs when:

a) the grapes don't get fully ripe

b) it rains during harvest, swelling the berries with water and diluting the sugars

c) persistent dampness causes rot in the vineyard

d) the grapes get overripe

e) an over-production of grapes

A great year happens when:

a) the grapes ripen fully and the production is relatively small

b) the fruit is clean and doesn't break down in the handling

c) the balance of fruit sugars, acidity and tannin are in harmony

One year can be very different from the next, especially in cool climates such as Burgundy, Loire, Germany, Austria, Ontario, British Columbia, Oregon and New Zealand.

Just because Bordeaux has a bad year does not mean that every other European region will also have a bad year. Local climates vary. Even within a given region, certain vintners can get better grapes than their neighbours depending on how they prune their vines, how much they pick and how long they allow their bunches to hang.

However, no one can be expected to follow the fortunes of every particular winery to determine the quality of a given year. Hence the need for vintage charts that provide very general indications of which years are good, which are mediocre and which should be avoided at all costs.

Here are the best vintages in the major regions. The finest are in bold:

AUSTRALIA

(red): 1990, 1989, 1988, 1987, **1986, 1985, 1983,** 1982, 1980

(white): 1990, 1988, **1985,** 1984, 1983, **1982,** 1981, 1980

CALIFORNIA

(Napa/Sonoma reds): **1992, 1991,** 1990, **1987, 1985,** 1982

(Napa/Sonoma whites): **1990,** 1989, **1986, 1985, 1980**

FRANCE

Alsace: **1990, 1989, 1988,** 1987, **1985, 1983,** 1982, 1981

Bordeaux (red): **1990, 1989,** 1988, 1985, **1983, 1982,** 1978, 1975, **1970**

Bordeaux (sweet white): **1989, 1988,** 1986, **1983,** 1976, 1975, **1971**

Burgundy (red): **1990,** 1989, **1988, 1985,** 1980, 1978, 1976

Burgundy (white): 1992, 1990, **1989,** 1988, **1986, 1985,** 1981, 1980, 1978, 1971

Champagne: **1989, 1985,** 1983, **1982,** 1979, 1976, 1975, 1973, 1971, 1970

Loire: **1990, 1989,** 1988, **1985,** 1983, **1971**

Rhône (red): **1991,** 1990, 1989, **1988,** 1985, **1983,** 1982, **1978, 1971**

ITALY

Chianti: 1991, **1990, 1988,** 1986, **1985, 1983,** 1982, 1981, 1980, 1978, 1975

PIEDMONT

1990, 1989, 1988, 1985, 1983, **1982,** 1979, **1978,** 1974

GERMANY

1991, **1990**, **1989**, 1988, **1985**, **1983**, **1976**, **1971**

PORTUGAL

(port): 1987, **1985**, 1983, 1978, **1977**, 1975, **1970**, **1963**

SPAIN

(red): 1991, **1989**, **1987**, 1986, **1982**, 1981, 1978, **1976**, 1973

ONTARIO

1991, 1990, **1989**, **1987**

BRITISH COLUMBIA

1992, 1991

HOW TO TELL IF A WINE IS "OFF"

This wine tastes "off," but what's wrong with it?

Wine is a living organism. Like human beings, it can get sick or it can get old before its time. Sometimes it can look and smell bad and not be nice to know.

Wine doesn't really like travelling. If it gets shaken up it can close in on itself rather like us when we get car sick. That's why you should let bottles that have travelled some distance rest for a month or so to "recuperate."

There are some faults you may come across when you open a bottle of wine that will be evident to the eye, the nose and the palate.

Appearance

Browning:

Both white and red wines will begin to brown when they age. The discolouration begins at the rim where the wine touches the glass. Eventually it will tint the entire glass. This condition is more apparent in reds than whites, but once you see browning it's an indication of aging or, worse, oxidation.

Oxidation happens when a wine is exposed to oxygen. Imagine the taste when you bite into a fresh apple. If you peeled that apple and left it standing in the air for half an hour or so it would begin to go brown and the taste would be dulled. That's oxidation.

An oxidized wine will have a characteristic smell. White wines smell like sherry, red wines of prunes.

Causes of Browning:

- Exposure to air because of faulty corks or wine left standing upright
- Wine stored in overly warm conditions or exposure to direct sunlight
- Wine unduly shaken up or continually subjected to vibrations. Wine kept beyond its natural life.

Cloudiness:

White wines should not be cloudy. Red wines have an excuse if they are old and you disturb their sediment. Otherwise, a healthy wine should be transparent or at least translucent (some reds are so dense you can't actually see through them).

A hazy wine signals a winemaking fault. The wine will taste metallic and bitter.

Cause of Cloudiness:

A chemical reaction between the acids in the fermenting grape juice and iron or copper.

Tartrates:

In some bottles, particularly whites, you may see a fine crystalline "sand" at the bottom. These are potassium bitartrate crystals that have been precipitated out when the wine is chilled down. They have no taste or smell.

Although this sediment looks unappealing, it has no effect on the wine whatsoever. There is no reason to send such a wine back in a restaurant since it is, ironically, a sign of quality. Most white wines are pasteurized and cold stabilized to ensure that they will have a longer shelf life and will be free of any organic acitivity. The better wines are not subjected to this treatment.

Smell:

Wines have a range of bouquets — not all of them may be pleasant. Off-odours tell you that there is a fault in the wine.
Beware of these smells:

Asparagus (cabbage):

Caused by too much use of sulphur in the vineyards or nutrient deficiency in the grapes. Also happens when a wine is left too long in the barrel or tank in contact with the dead yeast cells (lees). Can also smell like garlic. Technical name — Dimethyl disulfide.

Barnyard (horsey):
The smell of a stable is due to the presence of yeast in the wine at the time of bottling. The yeast cells react with the residual sugar in the wine diminishing the fruit and varietal character of the grape. Technical name — Brettanomyces. Winemakers in California call it, familiarly, Brett.

Burnt match head:
The presence of sulphur in the wine. Sulphur is used extensively in the vineyard and the cellar as an anti-oxidant and anti-bacterial agent. Our noses can only detect it in wine at around 30 parts per million.

Corky:
The smell of cork mold or a dirty barrel. Technical name — 2,4,6-trichloranisole.

Dill pickle (sauerkraut):
A soil-like odor caused by bacteria during fermentation when insufficient SO_2 is used.

Egg salad (rotten eggs):
The presense of hydrogen sulphide in the wine. Excess sulphur dust in the vineyards will combine with yeast to produce various sulphides.

Geranium:
The flowers may look pretty, but their smell in a wine tells you that there was a problem during fermentation creating a micro-organism that smells intensely of geranium leaves.

Milky (sour milk):
Lactic acid, one of the many acids in wine, also is found in milk. An overabundance makes a wine that should be fresh and fruity smell like buttermilk.

Nail polish remover (airplane glue):
The presence of high amounts of volatile acidity spells a sick wine.
It will taste of balsamic vinegar. Technical name — Ethyl acetate.

Musty:
Can be caused by dirty barrels, rotten grapes, a spoiled cork or
sloppy cellar practices.

Rubber:
Caused by the breakdown on sulphur in older wines.

Sherry:
The smell of sherry occurs, more often in white wines, with the
growth of surface yeast. Technical name — Acetaldehyde.

Vegetal:
A vineyard bacteria (Pediococcus) that imparts a vegetal character
to the wine and a taste of dirty socks. Found in a lot of red
Burgundies.

Bad Smells/Bad Taste

You should be able to detect a potential unpleasant taste on
the nose. That is why waiters will hand you the cork and
pour you a sample of the wine before they serve it to the
table. "If it smells off don't put it to your lips" should be the
rule.

CHAPTER 7

Wine and Food

*L*earning to match food and wine is not as intimidating as it might seem at first blush. It is not a jigsaw puzzle; there is no one perfect wine for a given dish which would exclude all others. And there are no hard and fast rules because everyone's palate is different and some people might prefer taste sensations that others find less agreeable.

There is also the question of the changing equation. A cut of red meat, or chicken or fish, is not to be matched to just one style of wine. The selection of wine depends upon how the meat is prepared — whether rare or well done — what herbs and spices are used, and whether the meat has been marinated or is to be served with a sauce.

Take steak, for example. To say you must have a red Burgundy with steak begs the question. How was the steak prepared? Was it marinated in olive oil and soya sauce? Was it grilled with pepper and flared with brandy? Is it to be served with a bernaise sauce or in a pastry shell? All of these different methods of cooking would call for a different style of red wine, if you want to be politically correct about it.

But wine and food are pleasurable experiences, so you shouldn't get anxious about what wines should go with what foods, to the exclusion of choice. The only rule is, You shouldn't have to interrupt your conversation to stare at the wine glass and wonder what on earth possessed the host to pair the wine of his birth year with frankfurters and beans.

There are some principles that will help you to choose wines for food, whether at home or in a restaurant. Basically, once you have asked yourself two questions, the rest is just fine tuning.

Are the food and the wine the same weight?

Match the weight of the food to the weight of the wine. A light dish demands a light wine. A hearty plate requires a full-bodied wine with lots of flavour.

How acidic is the wine?

Acid cleanses the palate of various tastes, including salt (shellfish, pickles, etc.), smokiness (smoked fish or meat) and greasiness (animal fat, butter, oil).

On the other hand, the fruit in the wine (its sweetness) reinforces the sweetness in the dish and works against saltiness, smokiness or greasiness.

Once you have determined if the dish you want to serve is light weight, medium weight or heavy weight, choose a wine style that corresponds. How do you determine the weight of a wine? Look on the label for the alcohol content.

Light-bodied wines	8% to 10% alcohol
Medium-bodied wines	10.5% to 12% alcohol
Full-bodied wines	12.5% to 16% alcohol

Now ask yourself how salty, smoky or oily is the dish? Consider the plate as a whole, not just the meat or fish. Vegetables can be highly acidic or, if glazed with brown sugar or honey, can be sweet-tasting.

Perhaps the saltiest, smokiest, oiliest dish there is is smoked salmon. It is very rich and concentrated in flavour which puts it in

the heavyweight class of food. Imagine having a soft, delicate, sweet wine with smoked salmon — it's enough to make you gag.

But match it with a full-bodied, dry white wine with lots of acidity and you have a marriage made in heaven. A dry Alsatian Gewürztraminer makes a wonderful partner. (Try it also with a dry sparkling wine, preferably champagne. Bubbles have a wonderfully cleansing effect on the palate.)

Where do you find acidic wines? High-acid wines come from cool growing regions.

France: Loire, Alsace, Champagne, Savoie, Jura

Germany: Mosel, Rheingau, Ahr, Franken

Italy: Trentino Alto Adige, Friuli-Venezia Giulia, Veneto

Austria: Krems, Wachau

Ontario: Niagara Peninsula, Lake Erie North Shore, Pelee Island

British Columbia: Okanagan, Fraser Valley, Vancouver Island

New York: Finger Lakes, Long Island, Hudson River

New Zealand: South Island

Fruity wines with less acidity come from hot growing regions.

Rhône

Languedoc-Roussillon

Australia: Victoria

California

Chile

South Africa

Sicily

Corsica

Sardinia

Portugal

Matching Grape Varieties with Foods

One of the easiest ways of matching food and wine is to consider the grape variety. If you have a particular wine available the following chart will assist you in making your pairing decision.

Red Grapes
Cabernet Sauvignon (red Bordeaux)

Full-flavoured red meats: steak, roasts, lamb, duck, game birds

Cheese: mature hard and ripe soft

Vegetables: onions, shallots, carrots, green beans

Herbs/spices: garlic, rosemary, thyme, dill, bay leaf, sage

Gamay (Beaujolais)

Light meat dishes, ham, sausages, hamburger, pizza

Cheese: light cream, Gouda

Vegetables: tomatoes, beets, carrots, peppers

Herbs/spices: ginger, mild chili, cinnamon, allspice, nutmeg

Merlot (St. Emilion/Pomerol)

Lamb, venison, game, turkey, meat casseroles

Cheeses: hard cheeses

Vegetables: eggplant, zucchini, squash

Herbs/spices: oregano, thyme, rosemary

Pinot Noir (red Burgundy)

Grilled meats, game birds, veal, roast chicken, rabbit, salmon

Cheeses: soft

Vegetables: tomato, mushrooms, beetroot, mushrooms, truffles

Herbs/spices: basil, cilantro, chervil

Syrah (red Rhône)

Highly spiced meat dishes, game, garlicky casseroles

Cheeses: mature, blue

Vegetables: ratatouille, peppers

Herbs/spices: garlic, black pepper, hot peppers, cilantro

Sangiovese (Chianti)

Casseroles, spicy sausage, tomato-based meat dishes, pasta, pizza

Cheeses: parmesan

Vegetable: tomato, mushrooms, truffles

Herbs/spices: oregano, thyme, marjoram

Zinfandel

Rich meat dishes, venison, game, roast turkey, spicy pastas

Cheeses: mature, blue cheeses

Vegetables: eggplant, peppers

Herbs/spices: garlic, pepper, fennel, cilantro

White Grapes

Chardonnay (white Burgundy)

Fish, shellfish, deep-fried fish, poultry, rabbit, veal, pork, cream sauces, egg dishes, snails

Cheeses: soft

Vegetables: potatoes, carrots, onions, leeks, squash, celery, corn, mushrooms

Herbs/spices: basil, tarragon, chervil, marjoram, mace

Chenin Blanc (dry Vouvray)

Shellfish, sole, chicken, pork, light cream dishes, soy dishes

Cheeses: Swiss, gruyère, emmenthal, St. André

Vegetables: corn, sweet peppers, carrots, cauliflower

Herbs/spices: basil, dill, mint, tarragon, caraway, nutmeg

Gewürztraminer

Oriental dishes, Thai, Japanese, light curries, smoked fish

Cheeses: Münster, Limburger

Vegetables: asparagus, Spanish onion

Herbs/spices: ginger, mace, cinnamon, nutmeg

Riesling (dry)

Fish, shellfish, game birds, pork, veal, Thai dishes, Chinese food

Cheeses: Edam, emmenthal

Vegetables: tomato, peppers

Herbs/spices: cloves, basil, sage, lemon grass

Sauvignon Blanc

Shellfish, fish, chicken, spicy sausage, prosciutto, vegetarian dishes

Cheeses: goat, feta

Vegetables: avocado, green beans, peas, asparagus, artichoke, peppers, fennel, salads

Herbs/spices: oregano, thyme, chives, dill, basil, cilantro, capers, chilis

Hot, Spicy Food & Wine

Highly spiced dishes can throw off the balance of many wines. If you want to match hot-tasting dishes, keep the following principles in mind.

* Choose wines with high acidity and some residual sugar (Vouvray, German Riesling, white Zinfandel, for example) rather than wines with perceptible oak flavours, evident tannin or high alcohol.

* For Mexican, Thai or light curry dishes select sweeter white wines, well chilled, such as Gewürztraminer or Riesling.

* Fruity reds with good acidity — Beaujolais and Valpolicella — when chilled will refresh the palate for mildly spiced dishes.

* For hot dishes that are also smoked, choose Zinfandel or Recioto della Valpolicella or Châteauneuf-du-Pape.

WINE SERVICE

What do you really need to serve wine at the table with style? There are on the market any number of devices, gadgets, glasses, decanters, thermometers, filters and other wine-related paraphernalia which are fun to own. But to enjoy wine, all you really need are some good glasses, a serviceable corkscrew and a decent decanter.

Glasses

Keep in mind that the wine is more important than the glass and you won't go wrong when it comes to choosing what you are going to drink out of. There are many beautiful glasses on the market — etched crystal, ornate stemmed, gilded and tinted in fanciful colours. Avoid them. They may look good on the table or in your glass cabinet, but they will ultimately detract from your enjoyment of the wine.

The watchword in selecting wine glasses is simplicity.

What you need is a plain, well-shaped glass with a long enough stem so that your hand doesn't have to touch the bowl (and warm up the wine) and a curved shape that captures and intensifies the wine's bouquet.

Elegant glasses have been designed that will show the faults in wines as well as those that flatter the wines. It all hinges on where the wine actually comes in contact with your tongue which registers various tastes in different parts. An Austrian company named Riedl has designed 24 glasses, each with a specific wine type in mind.

A well-equipped household needs only three shapes. For the starting wine drinker you can even make do with a single glass.

White wine: Clear, slim, elongated tulip shape with a longish stem, not too thick around the rim.

Red wine: Clean, rounded bowl whose aperture is smaller than the circumference of the belly.

Sparkling wine: Tall, slender, flute shape narrowing at the aperture. Long stem, thin glass.

Single all-purpose glass: The standard tasting glass tulip shape, elegant bowl that narrows towards the aperture.

Corkscrews

There are many corkscrews on the market and most of them aren't worth a damn. Avoid:

* Devices with needles that involve injecting or pumping air into the wine to force out the cork. Any flaw in the bottle neck could cause it to break under the added pressure.

* Butterfly ratchet-style openers. They break down easily.

* Plastic corkscrews usually found in hotel bedrooms.

* Simple T-shaped corkscrews. Too difficult to use.

* The Ah-So. A two-bladed device with a metal grip that slides down between the cork and the bottle neck. Most people end up pushing the cork into the bottle rather than extracting it.

Choose:

* The lever corkscrew with a blade for cutting capsules, used by waiters everywhere.

* The Screwpull — more expensive, but it has an infallible way of uncorking a bottle.

When selecting a corkscrew, make sure that the helix (the metal spiral) is long enough (at least two inches) to pierce far enough into a Bordeaux cork to withdraw it without breakage. And if possible, it should be teflon-coated for ease of insertion. The helix should be thin, shaped in a circular spiral and not be sharp-edged. A thick helix with a cutting edge will force the cork apart and may cause it to break up.

Make sure that the point of the helix is sharp and that the blade is kept sharp at all times.

Opening a Bottle of Wine Using the Lever Corkscrew

Most wines these days have capsules that are made of plastic or tin foil. They are also engineered so that you can remove them with your fingers. But older wines will have lead capsules which have to be removed so that the wine does not come in contact with them.

Step 1:
Cut the capsule in a circular motion below the lip of the bottle and remove.

Step 2:
Wipe the neck of the bottle with a cloth. There may be some debris or harmless mold under the capsule.

Step 3:
Insert the point of the helix into the centre of the cork and slowly work it down with a circular motion of the wrist. Ensure that the helix is going in straight. Continue turning until you see only one circle of the helix left. Avoid letting the point break through the bottom of the cork as this will create debris on the surface of the wine.

Step 4:
Clamp the lever against the lip of the bottle and hold it in place. Slowly lever the handle upwards. As the cork begins to rise (and with it your elbow), change the position of your hand so that you are gripping the corkscrew with your thumb pointing upward. This will make you more comfortable for the final removal of the cork. Continue the gentle upward pressure. Once removed, use the cork to wipe off any debris around the mouth of the bottle.

Pouring

Adequate measures

As a host, you want to appear generous. But avoid the temptation to fill a wine glass too full. Pour to a maximum of two-thirds of the capacity of the glass. This will allow your guests to swirl the wine (to get more of its bouquet) and they won't give their noses a bath when they go to drink. Four to six ounces is an adequate measure.

Pouring Champagne

All sparkling wines should be poured one-third of a glass at a time to allow the initial bubbles to settle. Otherwise, the wine will overflow.

No dripping

To avoid that last drop falling on the tablecloth, give the bottle a half turn with your wrist just as you finish pouring a glass. This will ensure that the drop falls back into the bottle.

Washing Up

No-smell glasses

Dishwashers can leave a soapy film on glasses which can adversely affect the taste of wine and can render sparkling wines flat. It is best to hand-wash wine glasses in hot soapy water. Rinse well and if possible leave hanging to air-dry. If not, use a clean, lint-free cloth or paper towelling.

Wine Glass Storage

* Don't store your glasses in the cardboard cases you bought them in. They will take on the "taste" of the carboard and you will have to rewash them every time before using them.

* Don't store them in your cabinet, bowl down. The entrapped air will permeate the glass with the smells of the cabinet.

* Wipe the glasses with a paper towel before use to remove any dust that may have settled on them.

Why Decant?

Although you may seldom have the occasion to decant a wine because of its sediment, the process of pouring any wine from one container to another has a beneficial effect. The gentle tumbling action introduces air into the wine and helps to unlock its bouquet and flavour.

This can be done by merely pouring the wine into a clean jug and then washing the bottle out with water if there is sediment and repouring back into the clean, dried bottle. Or you can buy a crystal or glass decanter which will look elegant on the table.

When buying a decanter, make sure the style complements the stemware you have chosen. Bring a favourite glass along to the store and see how it looks beside the decanter.

Decanting

Watching a sommelier in a fancy restaurant decanting a bottle of wine over a candle flame can be very dramatic, but there are very few occasions when you will have to do this yourself. There are only three reasons why decanting might be necessary:

1. To remove the wine from its sediment. Only older reds will throw a sediment, although if the sight of "wine diamonds" — potassium bitartrate crystals — in your white wine offends you, you might like to clean it up by decanting.

2. To aerate a wine and bring it more quickly to room temperature.

3. For the aesthetic reason of appreciating the look of a fine red wine in a glass decanter.

Decanting Procedure

Step 1:

Let the bottle stand upright for a few hours to ensure that all the sediment has settled to the bottom of the bottle.

Step 2:

Carefully remove the entire capsule and wipe the neck clean so that you will have a clear view of the wine as it flows from the bottle into the decanter.

Step 3:

Light a candle or stand a flashlight on the table so that the beam points to the ceiling.

Step 4:

Take a clean, dry decanter or jug with a capacity larger than the bottle. Place it next to the candle or flashlight.

Step 5:

Lift the bottle in your pouring hand without disturbing the sediment and lift the decanter with the other. Angle the bottle over the flame or beam so the light shines through the neck of the bottle.

Step 6:

Make sure you are comfortable and will not have to answer the phone or the demands of children because once you start you have to finish; otherwise, the wine will get cloudy if the pouring is interrupted. Begin pouring gently into the decanter. Do not let the flow "glug, glug" into the decanter as the movement will eventually stir up the sediment. Using a steady, even flow, keep pouring until you see the beginnings of the sediment moving towards the neck. Stop at this point. You should have only an inch or two of wine left in the bottle and the wine in the decanter should be crystal clear.

Step 7:

If you want to pre-taste the decanted wine, use a coffee filter in a wine glass to strain the remains in the bottle. You can also use this portion for cooking.

(If you were to pour the residue in the bottle straight into a glass, you would understand how decanting helps a wine that has thrown a sediment. First, the wine is muddy and dull. Second it smells slightly bitter and earthy. And third, if you taste it, it will be very bitter and astringent — unlike the same wine in the decanter. The reason is, the sediment is tannin that has been precipitated out over time. By decanting you are removing that unpleasant tasting compound from the wine and ensuring that it looks bright and lively in the glass.)

Cleaning Decanters

Lead crystal decanters look beautiful on the table, but they are difficult to clean after being stained with red wine. Swish them out with bicarbonate of soda (baking powder) dissolved in hot water. For stubborn stains substitute sand which has an abrasive effect.

Leaving wine in decanters for a period of weeks can leach out lead. If you are going to use a lead crystal decanter, don't keep your wine in it for more than a few days. Alcohol can extract molecules of lead over a period of time.

Wine Serving Temperatures

Wine served at the wrong temperature can spoil the taste. A red that reaches room temperature of 72 degrees Fahrenheit (22 degrees Celsius) will taste flabby as the alcohol starts to evaporate. A white served too cold (frosting the glass) will lose its flavour. Chilling a wine lowers the perception of sweetness and emphasises the acidity, making the wine taste fresher.

What then are the proper serving temperatures for wine?

Generally speaking, take account of the weather. On a cool day your whites and reds can be slightly warmer. On a hot day serve whites well-chilled and reds at cellar temperature.

Red wines:

Optimum serving temperature 60 to 68 degrees Fahrenheit (16 to 20 degrees Celsius).

Serve fruity reds such as Beaujolais and Pinot Noirs (red Burgundy) at cooler temperatures than Cabernet Sauvignon (red Bordeaux) or Rhône.

Serve older wines on the cooler side.

White wines:

Optimum serving temperature 45 to 50 degrees Fahrenheit (7 to 10 degrees Celsius).

The sweeter the wine, the lower the temperature but not so cold that the glasses get frosted up. The same holds true for sparkling wines and champagnes.

Rosé wines:

Optimum serving temperature 45 to 50 degrees Fahrenheit (7 to 10 degrees Celsius).

Cooler for semi-sweet rosés and those that sparkle.

Chilling Time

It does not take long for a wine to chill down to the required temperature. Twenty minutes in an ice bucket half-filled with water and a couple of trays of ice cubes (so that the level is neck-high on the bottle) is sufficient time.

Thirty minutes standing in a fridge will bring the wine down to 50 degrees Fahrenheit (10 degrees Celsius).

For fruity red wines that you want to chill lightly (Beaujolais, Valpolicella), 10 minutes in an ice bucket or 15 to 20 minutes in the fridge will suffice. Then remove the wine from the cold and let it stand on the table (on a mat or plate so that you don't mark the surface).

WINE IN THE KITCHEN

The cunning cook will always have a glass of wine at his or her elbow to refresh, inspire and enjoy. And if some of that wine gets tipped into the frying pan or cooking pot, so much the better for the ultimate delight of the guests.

The uses of wine in food are manifold. You can employ wine to marinate meat, game and poultry. You can splash some into the sauce, beef up a soup, freshen up fruit and berries, whip up a sabayon, heat up a fondue or prepare a sherbert. Wine will also jazz up jams, jellies, chutnies and preserves. And you can use wine in salad dressing instead of vinegar, especially if you want to serve wine with the salad.

When you cook with wine, here are some pointers to keep in mind.

Rule No. 1:

Don't add any wine to a dish that you would not drink from a glass. There is a very human tendency to want to save a wine that tastes a little "off" and use it for cooking. But why add a flavour to food that you've already decided you don't like in the wine? So make sure that your cooking wine is sound.

- Keep in mind you are not adding alcohol to a dish if the wine is heated for a few minutes in the cooking process. The alcohol will evaporate off because it has a lower boiling point than water. Water boils at 100 degrees Celsius (212 Fahrenheit) while alcohol boils at 77 degrees Celsius (173 Fahrenheit). (Alcohol also has a lower freezing point than water.)

- Never boil wine by itself. It can burn and introduce harsh flavours into your dish. Allow it to simmer gently.

- When you substitute wine for vinegar in salad dressing, simmer the wine and reduce by half. Then allow to cool before you mix with oil and condiments. Heating wine concentrates its flavour and sweetness as well as its acidity.

- For best results, choose cooking wines that have lots of flavour. Delicate, old or subtle wines get lost in rich dishes.

- If you add the wine at the beginning of preparation, you will cook away the flavour. Add the wine towards the end of the cooking time.

- Don't add raw wine to a dish just prior to serving. It will not have had a chance to meld with the other tastes and the alcohol will be apparent.

- Don't add more than the recipe calls for. You want to be generous with your guests, but spiking a dish with too much wine will add acidity to the food.

- Don't use your best wines for cooking. If you want to keep the heel of a bottle for kitchen use, pour enough olive oil into the bottle to cover the surface and exclude air. The wine will keep for a week this way. The oil will separate from the wine when you come to pour it out slowly.

- You can also store wine for cooking by freezing it as ice cubes.

- If you are decanting an old wine for dinner, use a coffee filter on the dregs left in the bottle and use the wine to deglaze the pan.

Wine Cooking Hints

Rule No. 2:
The acidity in wine can cause milk, cream and eggs to curdle. To avoid this, add the wine you have previously reduced and cooled towards the end of the preparation.

Rule No. 3:
Wines have their own flavours that can augment those in a dish:

- Beaujolais: Cherry
- Cabernet Sauvignon: Cassis
- Chardonnay: Apple-pear
- Oaky Californian and Australian Chardonnays: Vanilla
- Pinot Noir: Raspberry

- Riesling: Lemon-lime
- Sauvignon Blanc: Vegetal flavours
- Syrah/Shiraz: Blackberry
- Sherry: Nuts

Rule No. 4:
Avoid putting wine directly onto vegetables. The acidity impedes the cooking process.

Rule No. 5:
Poaching fruit in wine makes an excellent (and easy to prepare) dessert. It works particularly well with peeled pears (try poaching them in Amarone!) and peaches, plums and cherries. If you use dry wine, add a tablespoon of honey or sugar. Sweet dessert wines such as Sauternes, port, marsala or madeira do not require any sweetening.

Rule No. 6:
One of the simplest and most dramatic of desserts is zabaglione: the egg yolks should be whipped to a foam before adding the marsala. (I can't resist giving the recipe here: 8 egg yolks beaten with 4 dessertspoons of caster sugar and the same amount of Marsala whisked in when the yolk and sugar mixture turns creamy and foaming.)

How to Cook with Wine
Marinades

- Wine tenderizes and flavours meat and poultry. Red wine will "stain" chicken and other white meats. Most red wine marinades need oil to help lock in the wine's flavour.
- For optimum results, reduce the wine to a glaze with the other ingredients in the marinade. This will concentrate the flavours. Allow the meat to marinate in the refrigerator

overnight (use a plastic bag or zip-lock pouch so you can turn the meat easily and get a uniform marinade). The absorption process speeds up if you marinate at room temperature.

- Don't marinate fish too long in white wine. The acidity will discolour the flesh and make it spongy.

- When you use the marinade as the sauce for the dish, make sure that it is not over-seasoned in the first place. You can always add condiments, herbs or spices if required.

Sauces, Stocks, Soups and Stews

- Don't overdo the the wine. The ratio should be one part wine to three or four parts liquid base, otherwise the wine flavour will predominate.

    Red wine will colour the sauce or stock. Tannin and acidity in reds help to balance the flavours of hearty meat dishes.

Stuffings

Wine is perfect for ensuring that your stuffing does not go dry. White wine is preferable since the acidity will complement the herbs and spices.

Cheeses

Wine and cheese are a natural pairing. When you make a cheese sauce, pour in a little white wine. The acidity will cut the fattiness of the cheese.

Adding "Raw" Wine

A dash of sherry in a soup just before serving is fine, but don't pour wine into stews, casseroles or sauces unless it has been pre-cooked. The alcohol will spoil the taste of the dish.

    Wine over desserts does work, especially fruit and berry dishes. Choose a sweetish wine like Asti Spumante or any of the other Muscat-based dessert wines.

CHAPTER 8

The 20 Questions Most Asked of Wine Professionals

1. What does it mean when a wine is rated "0", "1", "2" or "3"?

Most provincial Liquor Boards use a numerical system called the Sugar Code or Sugar Index to give the residual sweetness of a wine; that is, the amount of unfermented grape sugar. This is expressed as a number from "0" up to the "20s". The lower the number, the drier the wine. Most dry wines are "0", but you will find that Brut Champagnes (the dry style) are usually marked as having a Sugar Code of "1". This is because grapes for champagne are picked when they are not quite ripe and are very high in acid (which is tart). The wine used to make Champagne would be too sharp to drink for most palates unless some sweetened wine were added after the secondary fermentation. Because of the high acidity, the sparkling wine tastes dry in spite of this "sweetening" dose.

No wine is completely dry. There will always be some grape sugars that cannot be fermented and will register in analysis as low as 3 grams per litre.

A wine rated as "0" on the Sugar Code will contain up to 5 grams/litre of residual sugar.

"1" = 5 grams to 14 grams/litre

"2" = 15 grams to 24 grams/litre

"3" = 25 grams to 34 grams/litre, etc.

What the Sugar Code tells you is only the amount of sweetness left in a wine. It does not tell you the amount of acidity which counteracts that sweetness. If you taste two "0"-rated wines side-by-side, such as Lindemans Bin 65 Chardonnay from Australia and Duboeuf Macon-Villages (also a Chardonnay), the Australian wine will taste decidedly sweet in comparison. The reason is that while both have less than 5 grams/litre residual sugar, the Lindemans Chardonnay has less acidity.

> In Quebec the sugar readings are done in words:
>
> Sec (dry) = up to 5 grams/litre
>
> Demi-sec (medium dry) = 5.1 to 12 grams/litre
>
> Demi-doux (medium sweet) = 12.1 to 50 grams/litre
>
> Doux (sweet) = in excess of 50 grams/litre

In Ontario's vintages catalogue, the wines are marked under the following system:

> XD = extra dry
> D = dry
> MD = medium dry
> M = medium
> MS = medium sweet
> S = sweet

2. When should I choose a "0"-rated wine over a "2"?

It depends upon the occasion, the company and what you're eating.

Many people don't like totally dry wines. A wine rated "2" by the Sugar Code would be styled as off-dry or medium-dry. You would experience a perceptible sweetness in the taste as in many German Rieslings, although the wine may finish dry. That is, the acidity will clean off the sugar and make the wine appear dry on the final taste.

"0"-rated wines go well with most foods, especially fish, seafood and vegetables. But spicy and highly flavoured dishes such as Thai and Mexican food require a little residual sugar to combat the "heat." In the final analysis, you should choose what you like to drink and not feel pressured to drink really dry wines if they don't appeal to you.

3. Why do some red wines give me an instant headache while others are never affected in this way?

People who suffer from red wine headaches are reacting to the tannin in the wine. Red wines contain more tannin than whites because the colour comes from macerating the skins of black grapes in the juice. This process extracts pigmentation, but it also draws out tannin from the skins, pits and stalks.

Tannin tastes bitter and it also feels astringent on the palate, but it gives red wine its potential of long life, softening as the wine ages and eventually — in really old wines — precipitating out as sediment.

There are also tannins in oak that are leached out during the wine's stay in barrels, especially new barrels. Tannin releases histamines in our bodies and, if you are allergic to histamines, you will suffer from the "red wine syndrome."

Certain red wines are made to have as little tannin as possible in order for them to be consumed when young and fruity. The obvious example is Beaujolais Nouveau that is produced by a method called "carbonic maceration." The grapes are not crushed but whole clusters are dumped into a stainless-steel tank. The weight of the mass crushes the bottom part and fermentation starts. The tank is sealed so that a blanket of carbon dioxide gas (the natural byproduct of alcoholic fermentation) settles at the top of the tank, excluding oxygen. The fermentation "leaps" from berry to berry, happening inside the skin. After four or five days the grapes are gently pressed and the resulting wine is low in tannin. This technique is used for all Beaujolais wines and is also practised in other regions.

Wines made by carbonic maceration will have less tannin than those made by the conventional method and may not cause as much distress to those who suffer from red wine headaches. Apart from avoiding red wine entirely (which would be a great pity!), guard against the effects by taking an aspirin before you drink a glass of red wine.

4. Am I less likely to develop a headache if the wine is more expensive?

Not necessarily. Certain people react to different elements in wine. You might be highly sensitive to sulphur products that are used in the winemaking process as anti-bacterial agents or anti-oxidants. Or you may be affected by tannin or egg whites that are used in fining the better red wines. Price, unfortunately, is no guarantee of immunity from reaction. But psychologically, if you buy an expensive bottle of wine you are more likely to be bound and determined to enjoy it and ascribe any unsettling effects to the food, the wine bore at the next table or cigarette smoke.

5. Why are some white wines a deep yellow colour and others are almost water white?

All white wines start out virtually the same colour when they are freshly fermented. The different shades of colour, ranging from pale straw to bronze (and in the case of really old sweet white Bordeaux to mahogany and opaque brown!) occur with age in the bottle or cask.

White wines gain colour as they age. A wine matured in oak will have more depth of hue than one aged in stainless-steel tanks because of the oxidation process. A sweet wine will take on more colour as it ages than a dry wine. The more sugar the grapes have at time of harvest will influence the colour of the wine. Low sugar will give a pale wine; high sugar a rich golden wine, especially if some residual sugar is left unfermented.

As a rule of thumb, sweet white wines will be deeper in colour than dry wines.

6. What does a "corked" wine mean?

"Corked" is a term used by the wine trade to indicate that a wine is "off" or oxidized. It smells swampy, like rotting mushrooms. There are many reasons why a wine may be corked. The bottle may have been badly stored in overheated surroundings or have been shaken up continuously due to the proximity of vibrating machinery (furnace, air conditioning unit). The cork may have dried out allowing oxygen to get into the bottle. There could have been rotten grapes in the press or a dirty barrel, an unclean bottle or a winemaking fault.

The term "corky," on the other hand, refers to the condition of the cork that has affected the wine. Chemical residue from the bleaching of the cork may set up a reaction which turns the wine. It is estimated that as many as 5 percent of all bottles sold in restaurants in North America are spoiled because of bad corks.

Cork comes from the bark of a tree and weevils can leave tracks which could prevent a hermetic seal, allowing air to get into the bottle and spoil the wine.

7. Is there much difference in taste or quality between an $8 bottle of wine and one that costs $12?

Certain regions can produce wine more cheaply than others. To make Cabernet Sauvignon in Chile, for example, is less costly than in Napa Valley because of the cost of land and labour. There is also the cost of equipment, especially the use of new barrels as opposed to old wooden vats. But if we were to compare the taste and quality of two Chilean Cabernets at $8 and $12 respectively, we might find a significant difference in quality. An $8 Chardonnay from France will not have the same intensity of flavour as a $12 bottle. The difference will be most likely that the cheaper wine was not aged in oak but in stainless steel, and that it comes from a region not renowned for growing Chardonnay.

While there is a difference in the price/quality ratio between regions (Chile, Bulgaria, Portugal, for instance, offer many wine bargains), within any given region you get what you pay for.

8. What kind of wine goes best with hot spicy foods?

Curries and dishes where hot peppers are heavily used make wine matching difficult, but not impossible. Choose white wines that are highly aromatic and have some residual sweetness (Sugar Code "2" to "4"). Serve them well-chilled. Grape types to look for are Gewürztraminer, Muscat and Riesling.

If in doubt, serve beer.

9. If you cooked a chicken in a red tomato sauce, would you serve white wine or red wine with the dish?

Plain roast chicken responds well to dry white or medium-bodied dry red wines, whichever is your preference. There are classic French recipes that feature chicken cooked in red Burgundy or in dry Alsatian Riesling. If you use tomato sauce in any dish, you are adding acidity to it because tomato is a highly acidic vegetable. You will need a wine with good acidity to match the sauce. You could serve a Sauvignon Blanc if you wanted white (presuming that you are spicing the tomato sauce with herbs such as basil, oregano or thyme and bay leaf) or — my preference — with a young red wine with good acidity, such as a Valpolicella, a Chianti or a Beaujolais.

10. If I could only pick one wine glass out of all the shapes available, what would be the most appropriate for the greatest variety of wines?

Many of the world's wine regions have developed glasses that best display the virtues of their wines. The size of the bowl, the diameter of the aperture, the length of the stem — all of these factors affect how the wine will smell and how it will taste when it hits your tongue.

The glass that is perfect for champagne won't do much for red Burgundy and vice versa. The closest approximation to the perfect glass for all wines is the ISO tasting glass which has an elegant tulip shape to entrap the wine's bouquet. The shape is fine for red, white and rosé wines; while not ideal for sparkling wines, it is certainly better than the traditional coupe glass that dissipates the bouquet, warms up the wine and doesn't allow you to see the rising bubbles. (See page 42.)

11. What temperatures should wines be served at? Can whites be too chilled?

Temperature is a very important factor when it comes to the enjoyment of wine. Let's take whites first. A dry white wine should be chilled but not as chilled as a sweet one. For dry whites, the optimum range is 7 to 10 degrees Celsius, slightly colder than the average cellar temperature. Half an hour in the refrigerator or 20 minutes in an ice bucket filled with water and ice cubes should bring the wine down to its requisite temperature. The same holds true for rosé wines.

Sweet white wines need to be chilled a little more to lower the perception of sweetness and enhance the acidity (or fresh taste). Serve dessert wines at about 7 degrees Celsius. There is nothing more sickly than a dessert wine served at room temperature.

Sparkling wines should also be served well-chilled, but do not put the glasses in the freezer as the "frost" in the glass will kill the bubbles.

You'll know if you are serving your wine too cold if it frosts the glass. Too low a temperature and you will not be able to taste the complexity of the wine.

Serve fortified wines such as sherry, madeira and white port lightly chilled, especially the sweeter versions.

Red wines should be served at the room temperature of a drafty English country home — not a North American apartment. The optimum temperature is between 18 and 20 degrees Celsius, slightly warmer than cellar temperature. A red wine that is served

above this range will begin to taste soupy as the alcohol starts to evaporate.

There are, however, certain light reds, such as Beaujolais and Valpolicella, that taste better when lightly chilled — 15 minutes in the refrigerator or 10 minutes in an ice bucket to reach 12 to 15 degrees Celsius.

12. Are there some wines rated "0" on the Sugar Code that go better with some dishes than others?

A dry wine rated "0" can have the perception of sweetness, particularly if it is grown in a hot region — California, Australia or Chile, for example. Sunshine builds up grape sugars which, when fermented, are converted into alcohol. High-alcohol wines generally have a "sweeter" taste than low-alcohol wines with the same residual sugar. This is because of the degree of ripeness of the grapes at harvest.

Another aspect that might reinforce a perception of sweetness in a given wine is new oak. The wine extracts a spicy vanilla flavour from the new wood. Winemakers will usually barrel-age and even barrel-ferment grape juice that has sufficient body and concentration of flavour to benefit from time in barrel. The leaner wines are aged in stainless steel or old oak barrels (which can no longer affect the taste). You will find that in cool growing regions — and particularly for the Riesling grape in Germany — the emphasis is on stainless-steel tank fermentation and aging in old barrels in order to retain the quintessential flavour and freshness of the wine.

So, not all "0"-rated wines are equal. As a rule of thumb, hot regions will produce full-bodied wines with lots of flavour and alcohol (giving a perception of sweetness underpinned by the flavours extracted from new oak), while cool regions will make fresh, lively wines that can be more enjoyable with food. The high-alcohol wines that are packed with fruit may bore the palate after a glass, whereas a lively, elegant wine will make you want a second glass.

Ultimately, the match of food and wine depends upon the dish you choose. (See Chapter 6.)

13. When it comes to buying wine as a gift for a host or hostess, what is a safe bet?

What you buy depends on whether you want your host to share it with you on that occasion (if so, bring a bottle of white wine or Champagne that you have chilled. The host, unless he's as thick as a barrel stave, will get the message), or whether the bottle is meant to be put in the cellar. Here are few tips:

1. If you want to have the wine opened at the meal you've been invited to, make sure you know the menu so that your bottle complements one of the dishes. Also, try diplomatically to find out what the wines to be served are so that you can fill in a gap. If the host is opening a bottle of Chateau Lafite 1961, your bottle of non-vintage Chateau Plonk is going to look like a wall-flower.

   This only works if you know the host well. To ensure that the wine is served, either drop around a few hours earlier and suggest that the host decants it an hour before serving, or bring it already decanted yourself.

2. Most people don't serve dessert wines, so a sweet wine to round off the meal would be much appreciated. But ensure you know how many people have been invited otherwise you will have to indulge in a little loaves-and-fishes magic with your half bottle of Icewine.

3. If it's an anniversary or a like celebration, try to match the vintage. Say the hosts have a new baby; bring a bottle of wine of that year to lay down (for the aging potential of different wines, see Chapter 6).

4. The safest wine to give a host or hostess is Champagne. No one can have enough of it. It's the only beverage alcohol you can drink with every meal and even before breakfast! Port is another surefire hit.

For lunch or brunch the most acceptable wines are dry or off-dry whites. Here are six suggestions that I would be delighted to receive from my guests:

- any white wine from Alsace
- Oregon Pinot Gris
- white Burgundy
- Rheingau Riesling Spätlese Trocken
- California Viognier
- Sancerre

For an elegant dinner, the emphasis should be on red wines. Any wine buff would appreciate one or all of the following six selections:

- Château-bottled red Bordeaux
- Domaine-bottle Burgundy
- California Cabernet Sauvignon
- Oregon Pinot Noir
- Italian Super-Tuscans (Sassicaia, etc)
- Spanish Rioja

A gift to the host is something that can either be kept in the cellar or consumed the next day:

- Champagne
- Port (vintage)
- Madeira
- Icewine
- Barolo
- A copy of this book

14. What is the "earthy" taste in wines, and why do some wines have it and others don't?

Grapes take on the taste characteristics of the soil in which they are planted. The roots of the vine suck up nutrients deep below the surface often pushing through layers of different soil substrata in search of water. The slate in a Riesling vineyard on the Mosel will give a characteristic flavour to the wine as will the chalk of Champagne vineyards and the limestone of Burgundy. Earthiness is first apparent on the nose.

The descriptor "earthy" can also apply to the feel of the wine in the mouth. Certain country wines made in the traditional fashion rather than with modern stainless-steel equipment and temperature- controlled fermentations can have a rustic quality. Reds are usually more earthy than whites, especially those from hot growing regions.

15. What kinds of grapes are used to make rosé wines?

Technically, any black grape can produce a rosé (pink) wine. The colour comes from the skins of black grapes, and the winemaker leaves the juice macerating with the skins for a matter of hours until the requisite hue is achieved. In cool regions where varieties such as Pinot Noir don't ripen fully, winemakers may opt to make a rosé rather than a red because there may not be enough colour in the grape skins. In hot regions, such as the Southern Rhône, the problem may be too much ripeness, so the grapes are picked when they are underripe to ensure they have enough balancing acidity.

The most popular grape for rosé in the Rhône where the famous Tavel and Lirac are made is the Grenache. In California, blush wines (the same technique with a touch of residual sugar left in the wines) are made from Zinfandel grapes.

Pink Champagne is made from the two black varieties, Pinot Noir and Pinot Meunier, or it can be a blend of white wine made from Chardonnay with a red wine produced from these two

grapes. Once blended to the desired colour, the wine then undergoes secondary fermentation in the bottle.

16. How long should you keep a bottle of wine in the refrigerator?

The ideal answer is the length of time it takes to chill down to the temperature at which you want to drink it. That means less than an hour. But the question has to do with storage rather than serving temperatures. Really, it depends on whether the bottle has been opened or not. An open bottle once recorked will last longer in the fridge than it would at room temperature. But if there is more air in the bottle than wine it will not last very long — a day at most before it starts to deteriorate. If you want to keep an opened bottle of wine in the fridge, take a clean half bottle and fill it as full as you can before recorking. By excluding as much air as possible you will prolong the life of the remaining wine. This way you can keep the bottle for a week or two.

An unopened bottle left in the fridge will deteriorate as well. The vibration of the compressor has an aging effect and the continued cold temperature will take its toll on the flavour. A wine that has been kept for two or three weeks in the fridge will taste flat. This is particularly true of Champagne.

17. What position should wine bottles be stored in for the short term?

Wines should be stored lying flat so that their corks are kept wet at all times. However, you will see in many wine shops that bottles are left standing upright. If you bring it to the clerks' attention, they will tell you that the turn-over is so fast that there is no time for the wines to spoil. That is pure laziness. What happens if a bottle doesn't sell? Frankly, it is better to be safe than sorry, especially with your own wines. Always store your wines lying on their side. The cork can dry out over a period of weeks and this will allow air to get into the bottle and oxidize the wine.

18. Is there a difference between how white wines and red wines should be stored?

Not really. Both should be allowed to rest on their sides in a dark well-ventilated room, free from dramatic fluctuations of tempera-ture, bright lights, vibrating machinery or chemical smells. Place whites nearer to the floor than reds as they last better if kept at a slightly lower temperature. Reds have more tannin that acts as a preservative. Whites have to rely on their acidity and alcohol.

19. Does allowing a wine to breathe make any difference to the taste?

Yes it does, for most wines. You can see this for yourself if you pour a glass of red wine and take a sniff and a sip immediately. Then wait half an hour to see what effect air has had on the wine. You will find that the bouquet is much more concentrated and the flavour has opened up. This dramatic change is not as perceptible in most white wines (it is in fine white Burgundy).

To air your wine, pour it into a jug or decanter before serving. Merely drawing the cork does not allow the wine to "breathe."

20. Is it all right for young children to have wine with meals and, if so, what is the right age to introduce children to wine?

If you visit a European family you will see that there is always a bottle of wine on the meal table alongside the bread and the salt. Wine is a staple food, not a product that has been restricted to government outlets. The family enjoys it together and the kids have a small tumbler usually mixed with water. When children are introduced to wine this way it does not become a forbidden fruit and they learn to respect it as part of the dining experience. I introduced my children to wine when they were eight years old because they were curious and wanted to know what it tasted like. I gave them a thimble-full mixed with water and as they grew I gave them a diluted glass whenever they asked for it.

Vintage Chart

Compiled by Vintages Purchasing Department for the Vintages
Classics Catalogue.

	1969	70	71	72	73	74	75	76	77	78	79
FRANCE											
Bordeaux Red	4	9	7	3	5	4	9	7	4	7	7
Bordeaux White	6	8	9	5	6	6	8	7	7	8	9
Burgundy Red	8	7	7	8	6	7	5	9	5	9	7
Burgundy White	8	8	7	7	8	7	6	8	6	8	7
Alsace	7	8	9	6	8	6	8	10	7	9	8
Cotes du Rhones	8	9	7	7	7	7	6	8	5	8	6
Loire							7	8	2	8	6
Champagne							9	8		7	8
ITALY											
Picmonte	7	8	10	2	6	9	5	5	6	9	8
Tuscany	9	9	10	5	5	9	9	6	9	10	8
Veneto	8	8	9	8	8	7	8	6	8	6	8
Friuli		7	8	7	7	6	5	8	6	8	9
GERMANY											
Rhine	7	6	10	5	6	6	8	9	4	6	7
Moselle	7	6	10	6	6	6	9	9	5	6	7
PORTUGAL											
Porto		8					7		10		
SPAIN											
Rioja	6	9	4	4	7	7	9	7	5	9	6
CANADA											
Niagara Peninsula											
AUSTRALIA											
Barossa Red	1	0	5	7	10	3	7	10	7	7	8
Barossa White		4	8	7	7	1	4	9	5	7	7
Hunter Red		7	3	6	7	6	8	7	6	7	10
Hunter White		6	2	4	6	8	7	8	6	7	8
UNITED STATES											
California Cabernet		9	8	6	7	9	7	8	7	9	8
California Chardonnay		8	7	6	7	8	9	8	8	8	7

The following key was used to evaluate the vintages:

10	Exceptional
9-8	Excellent
7	Very Good
6-5	Good
4-0	Fair to Poor

80	81	82	83	84	85	86	87	88	89	90	91	92	93
5	7	9	9	5	8	8	6	8	9	9	5	5	6
7	7	7	7	6	7	7	7	8	8	8	7	6	6
6	7	5	8	6	7	6	7	9	8	10	6	6	7
7	7	8	8	6	7	6	6	7	8	8	6	8	6
7	7	8	10	6	9	7	7	8	9	9	6	7	8
8	7	7	8	7	9	7	7	9	9	9	5	5	4
5	6	8	9	7	7	7	7	8	9	10	5	6	7
7	8	9	7		9	7			8	7			
7	6	9	8	6	9	8	7	8	8	9	5	5	8
7	6	7	7	6	8	8	7	9	6	9	5	7	8
7	7	8	7	6	8	8	7	7			6	6	5
5	7	9	8	6	8	9	7	7	9	9	6	6	5
6	8	6	8	6	7	6	6	8	9	9	6	7	5
7	8	7	8	6	7	6	6	8	9	9	6	7	6
6		7	7		9						8		
7	9	10	7	6	7	7	9	7	7	8	5	6	6
8	3	6	7	4	9	4	7	9	6	8	9	5	9
7	4	8	4	10	9	7	8	9	9	9	9	6	5
7	5	8	4	10	10	5	8	7	9	7	8	6	6
8	7	8	8	8	7	7	7	7	7	5	8	6	5
8	6	8	8	8	8	8	8	5	9	7	8	6	6
9	8	9	8	7	8	8	8	6	6	9	8	7	6
8	9	8	9	8	9	8	8	7	6	8	8	8	6

Index

Notes

Notes

Notes

Notes

Notes

Notes

Notes

Notes

ABOUT THE AUTHOR

*T*ony Aspler is the most wide-
ly-read wine writer in Canada
and has won numerous awards for his work. He has been active
in the international wine world since 1964. He received his basic
wine education in London, England, at Grant's of St. James' Wine
School (passed with distinction).

As a consultant and wine judge, he makes frequent trips to
the vineyards and wine fairs of Europe and the New World, and is
recognised as the leading authority on Canadian wines.

Tony Aspler has been the wine columnist of *The Toronto Star*
since 1980 and is currently executive editor of Canada's national
wine magazine, *Winetidings*.

Apart from his own wine books, he has contributed to Jancis
Robinson's *The Oxford Companion to Wine* and the *Larousse
Encyclopedia of Wine*.

He is also the author of seven novels, including *Titanic* and
Blood is Thicker Then Beaujolais (featuring the wine-writer detective Ezra Brant).